Influential Muslim Power in the 21st Century:

Book 2

Beyond the Gulf – Emerging Blocs-

Dr. Shaikh Mohammad Shahriyar Wahab

Copyright Notice

© 2025 Dr. Shaikh Mohammad Shahriyar Wahab

All rights reserved.

No part of this book may be reproduced, stored in a retrieval system, transmitted, or distributed in any form or by any means — electronic, mechanical, photocopying, recording, or otherwise — without the prior written permission of the copyright holder, Dr. Shaikh Mohammad Shahriyar Wahab.Legal action may be taken for any unauthorised use, reproduction, or distribution of this book or any part thereof.

Legal Notice

This book is an original work by Dr. Shaikh Mohammad Shahriyar Wahab. All rights are exclusively reserved by the author.

No content from this publication, whether in part or whole, including any text, graphics, illustrations, or referenced material, may be copied, adapted, published, or used in any manner without obtaining formal permission in writing from the author.

Photo

Adobe

Disclaimer

This book represents the views, opinions, and understanding of Dr. Shaikh Mohammad Shahriyar Wahab, developed through his personal research, study, and reflections.

This book is not intended to serve as an official religious reference, scholarly authority, or final verdict on any religious matter or personality. It is a collection of thoughts and analysis based on the author's personal comprehension of the topics discussed.

Readers are strongly encouraged to exercise their own judgment, consult other qualified scholars, and form their own understanding — especially on sensitive matters concerning religion, faith, and personalities mentioned within this work.

Neither the author nor the publisher shall be held responsible for any interpretation, application, or

Dr. Shaikh Mohammad Shahriyar Wahab

consequences arising from the use of the material in this book.

To my beloved mother, Syeda Quamrun Naher, who, by the mercy of Allah, has reached the blessed age of 80 in the year 2025.

Her unwavering prayers, boundless love, and quiet strength have been the cornerstone of my life's journey.

She is my greatest blessing in this world.

May Allah grant her continued health, peace, and the highest place in Jannah.

Contents

Disclaimer 1
Preface 9
Introduction 11
1. Introduction: The Muslim World in 2025: A Shifting Geopolitical Landscape 13
   The Evolving Global Order and the Rise of NonWestern Alliances 15
   Defining the Scope Key Players and Methodological Approaches 21
   Historical Context Tracing the Evolution of Muslim States in the 20th and 21st Centuries ... 27
   Religious Identity and Political Stability Navigating the Interplay 33
   Economic Development and Social Challenges A Comparative Analysis 39
2. Egypt: Navigating Regional Instability and Internal Reform 45
   The Sisi Era Consolidating Power and Addressing Security Concerns 47
   Economic Reform and Development Challenges Balancing Growth and Equity 53
   Religious Identity and Political Participation A Complex Relationship 59
   Foreign Policy and Regional Roles Balancing Regional Alliances 65
   Military Modernization and National Security Safeguarding National Interests 71
3. Türkiye: Balancing Domestic Politics and Regional Ambitions 77
   Erdogans Legacy Consolidating Power and Redefining Turkish Identity 79
   Economic Transformation and Development Challenges Navigating Global Markets 85

Religious Identity and Secularism A Contested Terrain	91
Foreign Policy and Regional Influence A Multifaceted Approach	97
Military Modernization and Regional Security Strategic Implications	103
4. Pakistan: Balancing Internal Security and Geopolitical Pressures	109
Political Instability and Security Concerns A Persistent Challenge	111
Economic Development and Poverty Alleviation Addressing Structural Issues	117
Religious Identity and Societal Divisions A Fragmented Landscape	123
Foreign Policy and Regional Relations Navigating Complex Alliances	129
Military Capabilities and National Security Regional Dynamics	135
5. Indonesia, Malaysia, and Nigeria: Diverse Trajectories, Shared Challenges	141
Indonesia Consolidating Democracy and Managing Diversity	143
Malaysia Balancing Development and Political Stability	149
Nigeria Combating Terrorism and Promoting National Unity	155
Comparative Analysis Common Themes and Divergent Paths	161
Regional and International Roles Engaging with the Global Community	167
6. Iran and Bangladesh: Unique Challenges and Emerging Roles	172
Iran Navigating International Sanctions and Regional Tensions	173
Economic Development and International Engagement Balancing Self Reliance and Cooperation	179

Religious Identity and Political Ideology A Unique Combination	185
Bangladesh Managing Rapid Growth and Addressing Social Issues	191
Foreign Policy and Regional Influence Expanding International Ties	197
7. Conclusion: Emerging Power Dynamics and Future Prospects	203
Assessing Emerging Power Dynamics within the Muslim World	205
The Evolving Influence of Muslim Majority Countries on the Global Stage	211
Challenges and Opportunities for the Future Forecasting Future Trends	217
The Role of Technology and Innovation Shaping Future Trajectories	223
Recommendations for Policymakers and Researchers Guiding Future Actions	229
Acknowledgments	235
Glossary	237
About Author	239

Preface

The year 2025 presents a unique juncture for understanding the intricate tapestry of the Muslim world. As non-Western alliances such as BRICS and the SCO gain prominence, Muslim-majority and Muslim-minority countries navigate an evolving geopolitical landscape. This book delves into the political, economic, and security dynamics of eight pivotal nations—Egypt, Türkiye, Pakistan, Indonesia, Malaysia, Nigeria, Iran, and Bangladesh—providing a comprehensive analysis of their distinct trajectories. The interplay of religious identity, political stability, economic challenges, and foreign policy choices within each nation is explored in detail. The analysis moves beyond a purely descriptive approach, striving to unveil the underlying factors that drive their evolution, offering a critical analysis of internal and external pressures. The careful selection of these eight countries provides a diverse representation of the Muslim world, facilitating a comparative approach that highlights common themes while acknowledging significant differences. The aim is to provide readers with a nuanced and timely understanding of this crucial region, avoiding simplistic generalisations and appreciating the complexity of its constituent parts. The book's rigorous methodology ensures a balanced and informed perspective, enhancing its academic value while maintaining readability for a broader audience.

Introduction

The Muslim world in 2025 presents a multifaceted and rapidly changing landscape. This book comprehensively analyses influential Muslim-majority and Muslim-minority countries, examining their historical evolution, political systems, economic development, military capabilities, technological advancements, and global roles. The study focuses on Egypt, Türkiye, Pakistan, Indonesia, Malaysia, Nigeria, Iran, and Bangladesh, representing a diverse spectrum of geopolitical contexts and internal dynamics.

The selection of these countries reflects their significant weight in global affairs and the vast array of challenges and opportunities they face. The book employs a comparative approach, allowing for the identification of common trends and unique national trajectories. A key theme is the complex relationship between religious identity and political stability, exploring how religious beliefs and practices intersect with political systems and societal structures.

We also examine the countries' economic development strategies, challenges related to poverty and inequality, and efforts to diversify their economies. Furthermore, the analysis sheds light on the countries' military modernisation efforts, regional security roles, and complex relationships with global powers. The rise of non-Western alliances, such as BRICS and the SCO, significantly alters the geopolitical landscape.

The book analyses how these alliances shape the foreign policy choices of the featured countries, as they navigate shifting global power dynamics and strive to safeguard their national interests. Ultimately, this study provides crucial insights into the evolving power dynamics within the Muslim world and the growing influence of these key players on the global stage, contributing to a more nuanced and informed understanding of a critical region in a rapidly transforming world.

Chapter 1
Introduction: The Muslim World in 2025: A Shifting Geopolitical Landscape

The Evolving Global Order and the Rise of NonWestern Alliances

The contemporary global order, long characterised by the dominance of Western powers, is undergoing a profound transformation. The rise of non-Western alliances, most notably the BRICS group (Brazil, Russia, India, China, and South Africa) and the Shanghai Cooperation Organisation (SCO), represents a significant shift in the global balance of power. These organisations, with their diverse memberships and varying geopolitical agendas, are reshaping international cooperation and challenging the established norms and institutions of the West. This shift has profound implications for Muslim-majority countries, many actively engaging with these emerging alliances to diversify their international partnerships and pursue their national interests.

Initially conceived as an economic forum, BRICS has evolved into a multifaceted organisation encompassing political, security, and development dimensions. The group's combined economic might, representing a significant portion of the global GDP and population, offers an alternative economic framework to the Western-dominated institutions like the International Monetary Fund (IMF) and the World Bank. This allure is powerful for many Muslim-majority countries that have historically felt marginalised or subjected to conditionalities within these Western-led organisations. The establishment of the New Development Bank (NDB) and the Contingent Reserve Arrangement (CRA) by BRICS provides a viable alternative source of financing and a safety net against economic shocks, reducing dependence on traditional Western financial institutions.

The SCO, on the other hand, primarily focuses on regional security and cooperation. Its membership includes several Central Asian states, Russia, China, and Pakistan, making it a significant player in the Eurasian geopolitical landscape. The SCO's emphasis on counter-terrorism, border security, and economic cooperation resonates with many Muslim-majority countries facing similar challenges within their regions. The organisation's focus on multilateralism and regional dialogue provides a platform for these countries to address shared security concerns and promote regional stability. This is particularly relevant in regions prone to conflict and extremism, where the SCO's cooperative framework can offer an alternative approach to security challenges.

China's Belt and Road Initiative (BRI) is crucial in the changing global order and its impact on the Muslim world.

This ambitious infrastructure project, encompassing land and maritime routes connecting Asia, Africa, and Europe, aims to enhance connectivity and foster economic integration. Numerous Muslim-majority countries actively participate in the BRI, receiving significant investments in infrastructure projects like ports, railways, and energy networks. This engagement offers substantial economic benefits but raises concerns about debt sustainability and potential geopolitical implications. Countries such as Pakistan, with its participation in the China-Pakistan Economic Corridor (CPEC), a flagship project of the BRI, have witnessed substantial investments but also grapple with managing potential debt burdens and navigating the complex geopolitical dynamics inherent in such large-scale partnerships. Similarly, countries in Africa and the Middle East involved in BRI projects must carefully weigh the economic benefits against potential risks related to geopolitical dependencies.

The rise of BRICS and the SCO, coupled with the BRI, provides Muslim-majority countries with a broader range of options in their international relations. This diversification reduces dependence on traditional Western partners and allows for greater strategic autonomy. However, engaging with these non-Western alliances also presents challenges. Navigating these organisations' diverse interests and priorities requires careful diplomacy and strategic planning. The internal dynamics within BRICS and the SCO, as well as the evolving relationships between member states, influence the ability of Muslim-majority countries to leverage these platforms effectively.

For instance, the varying governance and human rights approaches within BRICS and the SCO present a complex landscape for Muslim-majority countries striving to balance their national interests with their commitment to international norms. The differing perspectives on democracy, human rights, and freedom of religion can lead to challenges in achieving common goals and consensus-building within these organisations. Moreover, the increasing competition between major powers, especially between the US and China, influences the dynamics within these alliances, creating opportunities but also potential risks for Muslim-majority countries caught in the middle of this great power competition.

Specific examples illustrate the complex interplay between these evolving alliances and Muslim-majority nations. Türkiye's strategic positioning, balancing its relationship with NATO and its growing engagement with both BRICS and the SCO, showcases the complexities of navigating this new geopolitical landscape. Pakistan's participation in the SCO, alongside its longstanding relationship with China, reflects a strategy of diversification and regional engagement. Indonesia's active role in various international organisations, including BRICS, demonstrates a commitment to multilateralism and engagement with emerging global powers. These varying approaches underscore the diversity of strategies Muslim-majority countries adopt in responding to the rise of non-Western alliances.

Furthermore, the impact on the global economy and security architecture is substantial. The shift in economic power represented by BRICS challenges the dominance of the US dollar and Western financial institutions. The SCO's focus on regional security provides an alternative counter-terrorism and border management approach. These shifts influence global governance, creating opportunities for reforms and greater inclusivity. However, the potential for increased geopolitical competition and rivalry must also be considered. The evolving balance of power may increase tensions and competition for resources and influence, demanding careful navigation from Muslim-majority countries seeking to maintain their national interests while contributing to global stability.

In conclusion, the rise of non-Western alliances like BRICS and the SCO marks a pivotal moment in the evolution of the global order. Their implications for Muslim-majority countries are significant, presenting both opportunities and challenges. By carefully navigating the complexities of these alliances, while also considering their own national interests and regional dynamics, Muslim-majority countries can leverage the opportunities presented by this shifting geopolitical landscape to achieve greater economic development, enhanced security, and increased global influence. The success of these countries in this new international context will depend upon their ability to adapt to the changing power dynamics, forge strategic partnerships, and effectively address the internal challenges that hinder their national progress and international standing. The future of the global order and the role of Muslim-majority countries within it remain profoundly shaped by the ongoing evolution of these non-Western alliances and their impact on the world stage.

Defining the Scope Key Players and Methodological Approaches

Defining the scope of any study encompassing the multifaceted political landscape of the Muslim world in 2025 necessitates a clear articulation of the key players and the methodological approaches employed. This book focuses on a selection of Muslim-majority and Muslim-minority countries, chosen for their geopolitical significance, diverse political systems, and representative nature of broader regional trends. These countries – Egypt, Türkiye, Pakistan, Indonesia, Malaysia, Nigeria, Iran, and Bangladesh – offer a rich tapestry of experiences, challenges, and opportunities within the broader context of the changing global order.

Several key criteria guided the selection of these specific countries. Firstly, their combined population represents a substantial portion of the global Muslim population, offering a representative sample of different regional contexts and cultural nuances within the Muslim world.

Secondly, their geopolitical locations and strategic importance within their respective regions make them pivotal players in regional and global dynamics. Egypt, for instance, holds a central position in the Middle East and North Africa (MENA) region. At the same time, Indonesia's archipelagic expanse and large population make it a key player in Southeast Asia. Similarly, Türkiye's bridging role between Europe and Asia and Nigeria's influence in West Africa are crucial aspects of their regional and global significance.

Thirdly, the chosen countries exhibit a remarkable diversity in terms of their political systems, economic structures, and levels of socio-economic development. This range ensures that the analysis captures the nuances and complexities within the Muslim world, rather than presenting a homogenised picture. Comparing countries like democratic Indonesia and theocratic Iran, or the relatively stable Malaysia with the politically volatile Nigeria, allows for a richer understanding of the diverse trajectories and challenges faced by Muslim-majority states. This diversity also necessitates a nuanced approach to analysis, acknowledging that generalisations about the "Muslim world" are inherently problematic and risk oversimplifying the complexities of individual national contexts.

The methodology employed in this study combines quantitative and qualitative research methods. Quantitative data, drawn from reliable sources such as the World Bank, the International Monetary Fund (IMF), and various academic databases, will be used to analyse key economic indicators, military expenditure, and technological advancements. This data will provide a robust foundation for understanding these nations' economic capacities and potential. Further, data on social indicators, such as literacy rates, access to healthcare, and gender equality, will illuminate the social progress and challenges each country faces.

Qualitative data, on the other hand, will be drawn from a diverse range of sources, including academic literature, government reports, news media articles, and policy documents. This qualitative analysis will provide context and interpretation to the quantitative findings, deepening the understanding of the political, social, and cultural factors shaping the trajectory of each country. The book will rely on rigorous analysis of existing scholarship to provide a nuanced understanding of the various historical, political, social, and economic forces shaping the contemporary realities of these countries. This approach is intended to provide a comprehensive picture beyond mere statistics to provide a robust analytical framework.

A crucial aspect of the methodology is the adoption of a comparative framework. This allows for identifying common challenges, shared patterns, and contrasting trajectories among the selected countries. However, the comparative approach must be applied cautiously, acknowledging each state's inherent diversity and uniqueness. Direct comparisons without considering historical contexts, cultural nuances, and specific political circumstances risk misleading conclusions. The analytical framework will explicitly address the limitations of cross-national comparisons, highlighting potential biases and acknowledging the unique contextual factors that may influence outcomes.

The theoretical framework guiding this research draws from several established schools of thought in international relations and comparative politics. Realism, with its emphasis on power dynamics and national interests, provides a valuable lens for understanding the strategic choices made by these countries in their interactions with other global actors. Liberalism, with its focus on international cooperation and institutional frameworks, is crucial in analysing the role of these countries in regional and international organisations, such as the Organisation of Islamic Cooperation (OIC), the Association of Southeast Asian Nations (ASEAN), and the United Nations (UN). Constructivism, emphasising the role of ideas and norms in shaping state behaviour, will be used to understand the interplay between religious identity, national identity, and foreign policy choices. The intersection of these theoretical perspectives provides a robust framework for understanding the complex interplay of factors shaping the political trajectories of these countries.

One of the significant challenges in undertaking a comparative study of such diverse countries is accounting for the vast differences in their political systems. The range extends from theocratic Iran to relatively secular Türkiye, from the multi-party democracies of Indonesia and Malaysia to the more authoritarian systems prevalent in other parts of the region. This diversity makes direct comparisons of political institutions, processes, and outcomes inherently complex. The study will address these challenges by carefully contextualising the analysis, focusing on specific institutional features and processes rather than attempting broad generalisations across vastly different systems. Furthermore, the analysis will draw on various indicators and datasets to capture the diversity of political realities, avoiding generalisations that might obscure significant country-specific differences.

Similarly, the economic landscapes of these countries vary significantly. Some are experiencing relatively rapid economic growth, while others are grappling with persistent poverty and inequality. This range necessitates a careful and nuanced approach to economic analysis. The study will focus on various economic indicators – GDP growth, poverty rates, levels of inequality, and foreign direct investment – to paint a comprehensive picture of the economic realities in each country. Moreover, the analysis will consider the impact of global economic trends, regional economic integration, and internal economic policies on each nation's economic performance.

Beyond the purely economic factors, the study will also consider socio-cultural contexts, including religious and ethnic diversity. The role of religion in politics and society varies significantly across these countries, ranging from the explicitly theocratic to the largely secular. The impact of ethnic and religious diversity on political stability and social cohesion will be analysed with care, recognising the complexities and sensitivities of these issues. This requires a deep understanding of each country's internal dynamics, the role of religious institutions, and the interplay between religious identity and political participation.

In conclusion, this study employs a rigorous and nuanced methodology to analyse the geopolitical landscape of the Muslim world in 2025. The selection of countries, the blend of quantitative and qualitative data, and the comparative analytical framework combined with a theoretically informed approach aim to provide a comprehensive and insightful exploration of this dynamic and complex region. While acknowledging the inherent limitations of any comparative study, this work strives to provide a rich and insightful account of the challenges and opportunities these key players face on the global stage. Carefully considering diverse political systems, economic realities, and socio-cultural factors will ensure a balanced and insightful analysis of the selected countries, avoiding generalisations and acknowledging the unique context of each case study.

Historical Context Tracing the Evolution of Muslim States in the 20th and 21st Centuries

Understanding the geopolitical landscape of the Muslim world in 2025 requires a deep dive into the historical forces that have shaped the present. The eight countries under examination – Egypt, Türkiye, Pakistan, Indonesia, Malaysia, Nigeria, Iran, and Bangladesh – each possess unique histories, yet share common threads woven through the tapestry of the 20th and 21st centuries. These common threads include the profound impact of colonialism, the rise of nationalism and subsequent struggles for self-determination, the complex interplay of the Cold War, the emergence of diverse Islamic movements, and the varied responses to globalisation.

The legacy of colonialism casts a long shadow over many of these nations. European powers' arbitrary drawing of borders during the scramble for Africa and Asia resulted in fractured identities and enduring political instability. Nigeria, for instance, inherited a complex ethnic and religious mosaic from British rule, a legacy that continues to fuel internal conflicts and political fragmentation. Similarly, the partition of India and Pakistan in 1947, a direct consequence of British imperial policy, led to immediate violence and ongoing tensions that continue to define the relationship between these two nuclear-armed states. Dutch colonial rule left a legacy of uneven development and lingering social inequalities in Indonesia. Despite its ancient civilisation and relative independence from direct colonial rule, Egypt experienced significant foreign interference during British influence and subsequent struggles with balancing regional power dynamics. The experience of colonialism shaped not only political structures but also economic systems, leaving many of these nations with weak state capacity, dependent economies, and deeply rooted social inequalities that remain formidable challenges in the 21st century.

The dismantling of colonial empires created fertile ground for the rise of nationalism. In many instances, nationalism was interwoven with religious identity, leading to the formation of states defined by both shared nationality and religious affiliation. The emergence of Pakistan as a separate Muslim state, fueled by the two-nation theory, stands as a powerful example of this phenomenon. However, the path towards nation-building was fraught with difficulties. Establishing stable governance structures in post-colonial societies, forging national unity amid diverse ethnic and religious groups, and building effective state institutions proved challenging. The struggles for national identity and the consolidation of state power were often marked by periods of political instability, military coups, and civil unrest, as witnessed in many countries under consideration.

The Cold War further complicated the political landscape of the Muslim world. The rivalry between the United States and the Soviet Union led to proxy conflicts, ideological battles, and the involvement of both superpowers in regional affairs. Some countries, like Egypt under Nasser, initially embraced non-alignment, but ultimately found themselves caught in the crosscurrents of superpower competition. Other states, like Pakistan, became close allies of the United States, while others, like Afghanistan, became battlegrounds for the superpower rivalry. This period left an enduring legacy of military interventions, political instability, and the strengthening of authoritarian regimes. The effects of the Cold War extend beyond mere political maneuvering. The arms race and the flow of weapons into the region contributed to internal conflicts and exacerbated existing tensions.

The latter half of the 20th century witnessed the rise of various Islamic movements. These movements, often motivated by a combination of religious revivalism, opposition to Western influence, and socio-economic grievances, profoundly reshaped the political landscape. The Iranian Revolution 1979 was pivotal, demonstrating the potential of religiously-fueled movements to challenge established political orders and fundamentally alter the relationship between religion and state. The revolution in Iran also had significant regional reverberations, inspiring and influencing similar movements across the Muslim world. However, the diversity within Islamic movements is substantial. Some advocated for a peaceful and gradual reform of society, while others embraced violent jihad as a means to achieve their goals. The response to these movements varied across different countries, ranging from state repression to the integration of Islamist parties into political systems.

Globalisation presented both opportunities and challenges for the Muslim world. Economic liberalisation, technological advancements, and interconnectedness promised economic growth and development. However, the effects of globalisation were unevenly distributed, exacerbating existing inequalities and creating new forms of social and economic stratification. Many countries grappled with integrating global capitalism into their existing economic structures. While some benefited from increased trade and foreign investment, others struggled to compete worldwide, leading to economic hardship and social unrest. This resulted in increased internal and international migration and further complicated existing tensions. The responses to globalisation also varied across countries, leading to economic and social consequences.

The historical experiences outlined above have significantly influenced the contemporary political landscape of the Muslim world in 2025. The legacy of colonialism, the complexities of nation-building, the impact of the Cold War, the rise of Islamic movements, and the varied responses to globalisation have shaped the political systems, economic structures, and social fabric of the eight countries under study. Understanding these historical trajectories is critical to comprehending the current political dynamics, the challenges these countries face, and potential trajectories in the coming years. This historical analysis will serve as the foundation for a more detailed examination of the specific political, economic, and social realities in each of the eight selected countries. It illuminates the diverse pathways Muslim-majority states take in navigating the tumultuous currents of the 20th and 21st centuries, leading to the complex and evolving geopolitical landscape we observe today. The following chapters will delve into the specific details of each country, building upon this historical foundation to offer a deeper and more nuanced understanding of their present-day realities.

Religious Identity and Political Stability Navigating the Interplay

The intricate relationship between religious identity and political stability forms a central theme in understanding the diverse trajectories of Muslim-majority nations. While Islam serves as a unifying factor across many of these countries, its interpretation and integration into political systems vary significantly, resulting in a broad spectrum of governance models and levels of stability. A simplistic approach that equates Islam with a monolithic political ideology would be a gross oversimplification, neglecting the rich diversity of Islamic thought and practice. Sunni and Shia divisions, the spectrum of interpretations within each sect, and the diverse expressions of religiosity within individual societies all contribute to a complex landscape where religious identity interacts with, shapes, and is shaped by political realities.

In countries like Indonesia, the world's most populous Muslim-majority nation, integrating Islamic principles into the political system has fostered a relatively stable democracy. Indonesia's constitution enshrines religious freedom, while simultaneously recognising Islam as the dominant religion. A pragmatic balancing act has characterised the state's approach: accommodating the significant role of Islam in society while maintaining a secular framework for governance. This is achieved through a robust system of checks and balances, a relatively independent judiciary, and a vibrant civil society. While challenges persist, including religious extremism and sectarian tensions, Indonesia's relative stability can partly be attributed to its success in navigating this delicate balance. The Indonesian model, however, cannot be readily transposed onto other nations due to variations in historical context, societal structures, and the specific dynamics of Islamic movements within each country.

Contrastingly, the experience of Pakistan highlights the potential pitfalls of a more explicitly theocratic approach. Pakistan's founding, based on the "two-nation theory," expressly linked national identity with Muslim faith. However, the attempt to create an Islamic state has been fraught with challenges, leading to periods of political instability, military coups, and ongoing conflicts. The interplay between religious identity and political power has often resulted in the marginalisation of religious minorities and the suppression of dissenting voices. While Pakistan has experienced periods of democratic governance, the influence of the military and the persistent tension between religious conservatism and secular aspirations have significantly hampered its stability. The complex interplay of religious parties, military intervention, and societal cleavages has led to a recurring cycle of political turmoil that underscores the challenges of integrating religious identity into a functioning democracy.

Egypt presents a different case study, where the relationship between religion and politics has undergone significant transformations over the past century. Under Nasser, the state sought to suppress religious expression that it deemed a threat to its authority, while simultaneously utilising religious rhetoric for nationalist purposes. This approach resulted in a period of relative secularism, albeit one marked by authoritarianism. However, the rise of Islamist movements in subsequent decades challenged this secular order. The Muslim Brotherhood's participation in the political process, followed by the military coup and subsequent crackdown on Islamist groups, demonstrates the precarious balance between religious identity, political participation, and state control. Egypt's recent history highlights the volatile nature of this interaction, explaining how a shift in the balance of power between religious and secular forces can lead to significant political instability and societal upheaval.

Iran's unique trajectory, marked by the 1979 Islamic Revolution, starkly contrasts with other models. The establishment of a theocracy in Iran fundamentally reshaped the relationship between religion and politics, leading to a system where religious leaders hold significant political power. While this model offers a certain degree of stability in maintaining a consistent ideological framework, it also leads to restrictions on political freedoms and limits on dissent. The interplay between the Supreme Leader, the Guardian Council, and other political institutions demonstrates the complexities of governance within a theocratic system and its inherent vulnerabilities to internal power struggles. The case of Iran illustrates that while a unified religious identity may initially appear to provide a basis for political stability, the concentration of power in the hands of religious authorities can potentially lead to restrictions on individual rights and create a system susceptible to internal conflicts.

Türkiye's experience offers another interesting example of the dynamic interplay between secularism and religious identity. Türkiye's founding father, Atatürk, established a staunchly secular state, aiming to sever the historical links between Islam and the political system. However, recent decades have witnessed a gradual re-emergence of religious influence in Turkish society and politics. The Justice and Development Party (AKP), under Erdoğan's leadership, has navigated this complex relationship by gradually expanding the role of religion in public life while maintaining a facade of secular governance. This pragmatic approach has led to significant political polarisation, with tensions existing between secular and religious segments of Turkish society. The ongoing debate surrounding the role of religion in education, law, and social norms highlights the continuing challenges in navigating the intersection of religious and secular ideals.

Nigeria, a nation characterised by its diverse ethnic and religious composition, provides a compelling case study of the challenges of managing religious pluralism within a politically fragile environment. The tensions between the Muslim north and the Christian south have frequently erupted into violent conflict, creating a significant obstacle to political stability. The struggle for resources, political power, and the influence of religious leaders further complicates the already precarious situation. The lack of consistent and effective governance and the prevalence of corruption only exacerbate the existing tensions, which the activities of extremist groups have further compounded. Nigeria's experience underscores the challenges inherent in integrating diverse religious identities into a cohesive political framework. It highlights how religious divisions can be exploited to undermine political stability and fuel societal conflict.

Malaysia, on the other hand, presents a model of relative success in navigating a multi-religious society. The Malaysian constitution recognises Islam as the official religion while guaranteeing freedom of worship to other religious communities. This approach allows for a certain level of religious autonomy while maintaining a secular framework for governance. However, the delicate balance between these elements has sometimes been threatened, especially during political tensions or social unrest. This experience underscores the need for inclusive and equitable policies that safeguard the rights of all religious communities and the importance of building a shared national identity based on principles of mutual respect and understanding.

Bangladesh's journey, marked by its history of political instability and societal struggles, presents a unique perspective on the influence of religion on politics. While Bangladesh maintains a secular constitution, the pervasive influence of Islam in the daily lives of its citizens shapes political discourses and societal norms. The country has experienced religious harmony and conflict, emphasising the unpredictable interplay between religious identity and political stability. The need for inclusive governance that embraces the country's religious diversity while guarding against the use of religion as a tool for political mobilisation remains a critical challenge for Bangladesh.

In conclusion, the interplay between religious identity and political stability in the Muslim world exhibits a striking diversity. While a common spiritual framework may offer a unifying factor, its interpretation and integration into political systems vary considerably, influencing governance styles and stability levels. Analysing the successful and unsuccessful integration strategies, ranging from Indonesia's pragmatic approach to Iran's theocratic model and Nigeria's struggles with religious pluralism, illuminates the complex factors at play. Understanding these varied paths is crucial for comprehending the current geopolitical landscape and predicting future trajectories. Each nation's unique historical context, societal structure, and the interplay of religious and secular forces shape its political destiny, underscoring the multifaceted nature of this critical relationship and its significance in shaping the future of the Muslim world.

Economic Development and Social Challenges A Comparative Analysis

The diverse economic landscapes of Muslim-majority nations present a complex tapestry of successes and failures, shaped by many intertwined factors. While some have experienced remarkable economic growth, others grapple with persistent poverty, inequality, and unemployment. Understanding these trajectories requires a nuanced analysis considering historical context, geographical limitations, political stability, and the state's role in economic development.

One crucial aspect is the level of state intervention in the economy. Countries like Türkiye, under the influence of the Justice and Development Party (AKP), have pursued a mixed-economy model, combining elements of state control with market-oriented reforms. While this approach has yielded periods of significant growth, it has also been criticised for fostering cronyism and hindering actual market competition. The AKP's focus on infrastructure development, alongside initiatives to boost domestic industries, has propelled Türkiye's economy to a considerable extent. However, concerns remain regarding income inequality and the sustainability of this growth model in the long term. The government's increasingly authoritarian tendencies and impact on economic freedom also pose significant risks.

In contrast, Indonesia has pursued a more liberalised market approach, resulting in substantial economic progress over the past few decades. Its vast natural resources, coupled with a relatively large and growing workforce, have fueled significant expansion in sectors such as manufacturing and agriculture. However, Indonesia continues to grapple with issues of income inequality and regional disparities in economic development. The concentration of wealth in urban centres and the persistent challenges rural populations face highlight the need for targeted policies to promote inclusive growth. Indonesia's success also rests on its ability to maintain macroeconomic stability and attract foreign investment, which can be vulnerable to external shocks and domestic political instability.

Pakistan's economic performance has been significantly hampered by political instability and frequent military interventions. Chronic budget deficits, low human capital, and infrastructure investment have contributed to persistent poverty and unemployment. While possessing substantial agricultural potential, Pakistan's agricultural sector suffers from outdated farming practices and inefficient irrigation systems, limiting its productivity. The country's reliance on foreign aid and its struggle to diversify its economy remain significant obstacles to sustainable growth. Efforts at privatisation have had mixed results, often hindered by corruption and bureaucratic inefficiencies.

Egypt's economic situation is characterised by a dual economy, with a relatively developed urban sector and a large, predominantly agricultural, rural sector. The reliance on tourism and remittances from Egyptians working abroad has left the Egyptian economy vulnerable to external shocks. Attempts at structural reforms to attract foreign investment and promote private sector development have faced significant challenges, hampered by bureaucratic obstacles, a lack of transparency, and an unstable political environment. High levels of unemployment, particularly among youth, remain a significant social and economic challenge. The state continues to play a dominant role in the economy, often at the expense of free-market principles.

The case of Iran highlights the complex interplay between international sanctions and economic development. Years of international sanctions imposed over its nuclear program have severely hampered Iran's economic growth. Despite possessing significant oil and gas reserves, Iran's inability to fully integrate into the global economy has restricted its potential. The sanctions have stifled foreign investment, limited access to international markets, and hindered technological advancements. Furthermore, internal political factors, including corruption and a lack of transparency, have compounded the economic challenges.

While efforts to diversify the economy are underway, their success will depend on overcoming internal and external obstacles.

Malaysia, a success story in Southeast Asia, has achieved significant economic growth through export-oriented industrialisation, strategic investments in education and infrastructure, and relatively stable political leadership. Its success in attracting foreign investment and diversifying its economy has enabled the country to maintain a high economic growth over the long term. However, rising income inequality and the challenges of transitioning to a knowledge-based economy remain significant areas of concern. Malaysia's relatively strong governance institutions and commitment to education and skill development have contributed to its economic success.

Despite its abundant natural resources, particularly oil, Nigeria struggles with significant economic challenges. Corruption, poor governance, and a lack of infrastructure have hampered its economic development. Dependence on oil has led to a lack of diversification and vulnerability to fluctuations in global oil prices. The country also faces significant challenges in improving its human capital, with high rates of illiteracy and poor access to healthcare limiting its overall productivity. The challenge lies in fostering a more transparent and accountable governance system and investments in education and infrastructure to address deep-seated socio-economic inequalities.

Bangladesh has experienced remarkable economic growth in recent decades, driven primarily by its ready-made garment (RMG) industry and remittances from overseas workers. Its commitment to exporting manufactured goods, alongside its relatively young and rapidly growing population, has resulted in sustained economic expansion. However, the country still faces poverty, inequality, and infrastructure development challenges, particularly in rural areas. Ensuring sustainable growth in the face of a changing global economic landscape and mitigating the risks associated with its dependence on the RMG sector are crucial for its future financial prospects.

Comparing these diverse experiences underscores the multifaceted nature of economic development in the Muslim world. While natural resources, geopolitical location, and global economic conditions play a role, the quality of governance, institutional effectiveness, and stable political environments emerge as pivotal determinants of financial success. The state's role in economic management, whether through interventionist policies or market-oriented reforms, significantly influences the economic development trajectory. The success of countries like Malaysia and Indonesia suggests the potential benefits of adopting a more balanced, market-based approach coupled with strategic investments in human capital and infrastructure. In contrast, the struggles of countries like Pakistan and Nigeria highlight the detrimental impact of corruption, political instability, and weak governance structures.

Furthermore, the issue of social inequality adds another layer of complexity to the economic challenges these nations face. The unequal distribution of wealth and opportunities frequently exacerbates social tensions and political instability, hindering overall financial progress. High levels of unemployment, particularly among youth, create social unrest and threaten political stability. Addressing these challenges requires policies that promote inclusive growth, create opportunities for all segments of society, and invest in education and skills development to improve workforce productivity. Investment in social safety nets, such as unemployment benefits and welfare programs, can also help mitigate the effects of economic hardship and reduce social unrest. The effectiveness of such programs hinges on a government's commitment to transparency, accountability, and equitable resource allocation.

In conclusion, the economic development trajectories of Muslim-majority countries vary considerably, reflecting the unique interplay of historical, geographical, political, and socio-economic factors. Understanding these diverse experiences and the complex relationship between economic development and social challenges is crucial for formulating effective policies and strategies to promote sustainable and inclusive growth across the region. The emphasis should be on fostering good governance, promoting transparency and accountability, investing in human capital, and diversifying economies to create resilience against external shocks and internal challenges. Only through a comprehensive and nuanced approach that tackles economic and social difficulties can these nations fully realise their financial potential and ensure a more equitable and prosperous future for their citizens.

Chapter 2
Egypt: Navigating Regional Instability and Internal Reform

The Sisi Era Consolidating Power and Addressing Security Concerns

The ascent of Abdel Fattah el-Sisi to the Egyptian presidency in 2014 marked a significant turning point in the country's post-Mubarak trajectory. His rise, following the tumultuous years of the Arab Spring and the brief presidency of Mohamed Morsi, signified a decisive shift towards a more authoritarian model of governance. Sisi's consolidation of power was swift and largely unopposed, fueled by a widespread public weariness with the instability and uncertainty that had plagued the nation in the preceding years. The military, already a powerful force in Egyptian politics, played a pivotal role in facilitating Sisi's takeover, effectively leveraging the existing power structures to secure his position. This wasn't simply a military coup, but a calculated maneuver to restore order and stability in the eyes of many Egyptians, who prioritised security over democratic ideals.

The early years of the Sisi era were characterised by a relentless crackdown on dissent and the systematic dismantling of opposition groups, particularly the Muslim Brotherhood. Mass arrests, trials marred by allegations of unfair proceedings, and the suppression of civil liberties became hallmarks of this period. The government justified these actions as necessary measures to combat terrorism and maintain national security, emphasising the threat posed by extremist groups both domestically and regionally. This narrative resonated with a significant segment of the Egyptian population, who viewed a strong hand as essential for overcoming the chaos and violence that had become a daily reality. However, critics argued that these measures were disproportionate, targeting not only genuine threats but also peaceful activists and political opponents, thus creating a climate of fear and repression.

Sisi's counter-terrorism strategy, while successful in reducing large-scale attacks, has relied heavily on security measures rather than addressing the underlying causes of extremism. The government's focus on military solutions, including extensive military operations in the Sinai Peninsula, has led to significant civilian casualties and raised concerns about human rights abuses. While the security situation improved in certain regions, the underlying issues that fuel extremism, such as socio-economic inequality, political marginalisation, and lack of opportunities, remained largely unaddressed. The security apparatus, empowered by the government, expanded its surveillance and control over various aspects of life, often encroaching upon the space traditionally occupied by civil society organisations. This resulted in a chilling effect on freedom of expression and association.

The economic policies implemented under Sisi have been marked by a significant reliance on foreign investment and substantial borrowing, coupled with attempts to promote private sector development. While some sectors of the Egyptian economy experienced growth, the overall impact has been uneven, with persistent challenges related to unemployment, poverty, and inequality. The government's focus on megaprojects, such as the new administrative capital, has absorbed substantial resources, leading to criticisms about prioritising symbolic projects over more pressing social and economic needs. The structural reforms, often promoted by international financial institutions, have faced resistance from various segments of society, leading to social tensions and protests. Despite these challenges, Egypt's economy has shown signs of resilience, primarily driven by remittances from Egyptians working abroad and a revitalisation of the tourism sector.

Egypt's foreign policy under Sisi has involved balancing between maintaining its regional influence, strengthening ties with traditional Western allies, and engaging with emerging global powers. Egypt's strategic alliance with the United States, built over decades, has remained important, despite occasional tensions regarding human rights and democratic reforms. The relationship with other regional powers, particularly Saudi Arabia and the United Arab Emirates, has significantly strengthened under Sisi. These

Gulf states have provided substantial financial support to the Egyptian government, lending economic and political stability. Egypt has also been involved in several regional conflicts, notably in Libya, demonstrating its influence.

The Sisi administration's human rights record has drawn significant international condemnation. The shrinking space for civil society organisations, pervasive surveillance, and lack of judicial independence have raised concerns from human rights groups and international bodies. The widespread use of arbitrary detention, allegations of torture, and the lack of due process in trials have been documented extensively, leading to numerous reports from organisations like Human Rights Watch and Amnesty International. The government's response to criticism has often invoked national security and the need to maintain order, effectively neutralising international pressure.

The interplay between the military, the state, and civilian society continues to define the political landscape of Egypt under Sisi. The military's influence extends far beyond its traditional role, encompassing various sectors of the economy and playing a significant role in shaping political decisions. This has resulted in a blurred line between military and civilian authority, raising concerns about the concentration of power and potential for abuse. Civilian society, though significantly curtailed, remains a force to be reckoned with, as demonstrated by intermittent protests and the persistence of underground activist networks. While Sisi has consolidated his control over the formal political structures, the dynamic between these forces remains critical to Egypt's political reality.

The long-term consequences of the Sisi era remain uncertain. While the government has achieved some stability and improved security, the cost has been high regarding democratic freedoms and human rights. Egypt's economic challenges, social inequalities, and the lack of political pluralism pose significant long-term risks. The extent to which the government can address these underlying challenges without resorting to further repression will determine the future trajectory of Egypt under Sisi's leadership. Furthermore, the international community's response to the human rights situation in Egypt will be crucial in shaping the country's future, particularly its relationship with key Western partners. The balancing act between national security concerns and the need for democratic reforms continues to be a defining characteristic of the Sisi era. Ultimately, the legacy of this period will be judged not just by its success in addressing security concerns and fostering economic development, but also by its impact on the rights and freedoms of Egyptian citizens. The extent to which the country moves toward a more inclusive and democratic system, while maintaining stability, remains a significant question for the future.

Economic Reform and Development Challenges Balancing Growth and Equity

Egypt's economic landscape under President Abdel Fattah el-Sisi presents a complex picture of progress and persistent challenges. While the government has implemented various reform strategies to boost growth and attract foreign investment, the impact on the population has been uneven, leaving unresolved deep-seated poverty, unemployment, and inequality. This disparity underscores the critical need for a more nuanced approach prioritising equitable development and economic expansion.

One of Egypt's most significant challenges is the persistently high unemployment rate, particularly among young people. The formal job market has struggled to absorb the growing number of graduates entering the workforce each year, leading to widespread frustration and disillusionment. This unemployment fuels social unrest and hinders long-term economic stability. While the government has launched several initiatives to address this issue, including vocational training programs and investment in infrastructure projects, these efforts have yet to yield substantial results. The lack of sufficient private sector job creation and the dominance of the public sector exacerbate the situation. Moreover, many available jobs often fall short of expectations in terms of salary and benefits, further contributing to the unemployment problem. While providing a safety net for many, the informal sector lacks the stability, benefits, and protection afforded by formal employment, perpetuating a cycle of poverty.

Poverty remains a deeply entrenched problem in Egypt, particularly in rural areas and marginalised communities. Despite government efforts to alleviate poverty through social welfare programs and targeted subsidies, the impact has been limited. The existing social safety nets often prove insufficient to address the needs of the most vulnerable segments of the population. The inadequacy of these programs is exacerbated by corruption and inefficient distribution mechanisms, often leaving those most in need without the support they require. Moreover, poverty is usually intertwined with other social issues, such as limited access to education, healthcare, and sanitation, creating a complex web of interconnected challenges that require a multi-pronged approach to address effectively. The growing gap between the wealthy elite and the impoverished majority fuels social tensions and poses a significant threat to social cohesion.

Income inequality is another pressing issue that continues to widen. The concentration of wealth in the hands of a relatively small elite contrasts sharply with the widespread poverty experienced by a large segment of the population. This disparity fuels social resentment and undermines social harmony and stability efforts. While government policies promoting economic growth are intended to benefit everyone, the benefits have not been evenly distributed, exacerbating existing inequalities. This unequal distribution has deep historical roots, rooted in land ownership patterns and resource access, further complicated by the current economic climate. Addressing this profound issue requires far-reaching policies to address the root causes of inequality, rather than merely addressing its symptoms.

The Egyptian government's strategy for economic reform has centred on attracting foreign investment and diversifying the economy. The government has actively courted foreign investors by implementing various reforms, including streamlining regulations, improving infrastructure, and promoting specific sectors for development. Significant investments have been made in infrastructure projects to upgrade the country's transport networks, energy infrastructure, and digital connectivity. While potentially beneficial in the long run, these investments have also absorbed considerable resources that might otherwise have been directed toward addressing more pressing social needs.

The Suez Canal remains a crucial source of revenue for Egypt, but the government's reliance on this single source of income represents a vulnerability. Efforts to diversify the economy and reduce dependence on the canal have shown progress in the tourism and information technology sectors, but significant challenges remain. While showing signs of recovery, the tourism sector remains susceptible to geopolitical instability and global economic shocks. The information technology sector holds promise for growth, but it requires sustained investment in education and training to cultivate a skilled workforce. The lack of adequate diversification presents a considerable risk to Egypt's economic stability.

The government's pursuit of economic reform has faced significant challenges, including bureaucratic obstacles, corruption, and a lack of transparency. These factors have often undermined the effectiveness of government policies and discouraged both domestic and foreign investment. The lack of an independent and robust judiciary and bureaucratic inefficiencies have hampered efforts to create a fair and predictable investment environment. Corruption, at various levels of government, has siphoned off resources that could have been utilised for development projects and social programs. Addressing these challenges requires strong political will and comprehensive institutional reforms to enhance transparency and accountability.

Specific examples of successful and unsuccessful economic policies are crucial to understanding the complexities of Egypt's financial trajectory. For instance, the development of specific export-oriented industries, such as textiles and ready-made garments, has shown some degree of success in generating employment and foreign exchange earnings. However, these industries often operate within a low-value-added framework, hindering the development of a more technologically advanced and high-value-added manufacturing base. Conversely, while boosting employment in the short term, some large-scale infrastructure projects have faced criticism due to cost overruns, a lack of transparency in procurement processes, and limited social benefits. The allocation of resources to these megaprojects, often at the expense of essential social services, has fueled public discontent and highlighted the need for more effective resource allocation strategies.

The impact of economic reforms on specific demographics has varied considerably. While certain segments of the population, particularly those employed in the burgeoning construction and tourism sectors, have benefited from economic growth, the most vulnerable groups—the unemployed, the poor, and marginalised communities—have often experienced limited or no improvement in their living standards. This disparity underscores the need for a more equitable distribution of the benefits of economic growth, ensuring that the benefits reach the most vulnerable populations and that economic reforms actively address their specific needs. This necessitates a more targeted approach to poverty reduction and social inclusion, going beyond broad-based initiatives to address different demographic groups' diverse and particular needs.

In conclusion, Egypt's economic reform efforts have yielded positive results, but significant challenges remain in achieving sustainable and equitable growth. The country's high unemployment, poverty, and inequality rates demand a more holistic and comprehensive strategy beyond attracting foreign investment and diversifying the economy.

Addressing these underlying issues requires a strong commitment to institutional reforms, improved governance, and social justice and inclusion policies. The long-term success of Egypt's economic development hinges on the ability of the government to create a more equitable and inclusive environment that provides opportunities for all segments of society to participate in and benefit from economic growth. The path forward requires a delicate balancing act: fostering economic growth while mitigating the risks of exacerbating existing social and economic inequalities. Egypt can achieve true and lasting economic prosperity only through a concerted and sustained effort to address these intertwined challenges.

Religious Identity and Political Participation A Complex Relationship

The intricate relationship between religious identity and political participation in Egypt is a defining feature of its contemporary political landscape. Understanding this dynamic requires navigating a complex interplay between the state, religious institutions, and civil society, a relationship shaped by historical legacies and contemporary power struggles. While officially adhering to a secular constitution, the Egyptian state has long maintained a close, albeit often tense, relationship with religious institutions, particularly Al-Azhar, the prestigious Sunni Islamic university. This relationship has been characterised by collaboration and control, with the state seeking to harness the influence of religious institutions while simultaneously limiting their political autonomy.

Al-Azhar's role has evolved. Historically, it served as a centre of Islamic scholarship and learning, largely independent of direct state control. However, the state's influence has grown significantly in recent decades, particularly under President Abdel Fattah el-Sisi. While Al-Azhar remains an important institution, its ability to independently shape religious discourse and interpretations has been constrained. This state oversight extends to selecting leading scholars and the content of religious education, ensuring alignment with the government's overall political agenda. The implications of this control are profound, influencing not only the theological interpretations disseminated within Egypt but also potentially shaping the broader political climate. This subtle yet powerful control mechanism limits the potential for religious institutions to become centres of opposition or dissent.

The rise and fall of various Islamic movements have significantly impacted the relationship between religious identity and political participation. The Muslim Brotherhood, for instance, transitioned from a relatively marginalised movement to a powerful political force in the years following the 2011 revolution. Their electoral success highlighted the significant political mobilisation potential within religious communities. However, this success was short-lived, as the military ousted President Mohamed Morsi, the Brotherhood's candidate, in 2013. This subsequent crackdown on the Brotherhood, accompanied by widespread arrests and the designation of the organisation as a terrorist group, fundamentally reshaped the landscape of political Islam in Egypt. The movement's suppression serves as a stark example of the state's determination to maintain control over religious-political actors and to preempt any challenge to its authority. This suppression, however, hasn't eliminated religious sentiment as a political factor; it has simply driven it underground, potentially making it more challenging to monitor and manage.

The government's response to the Muslim Brotherhood's rise and subsequent suppression has involved a multi-pronged strategy. This strategy includes directly suppressing the Brotherhood and broader efforts to regulate religious discourse and institutions. This has entailed tighter control over mosques, the appointment of state-sanctioned imams, and stricter regulation of religious education. These measures are aimed at curbing the influence of what the government views as extremist ideologies while simultaneously attempting to co-opt and control more moderate religious expressions. The effectiveness of this strategy remains a subject of debate. While it has successfully weakened the Brotherhood's political presence, it has also created a climate of fear and self-censorship, potentially silencing legitimate religious expression and hindering genuine religious freedom.

Beyond the Muslim Brotherhood, other smaller Islamic movements continue to operate within Egypt, often navigating a delicate balance between expressing their religious views and avoiding state repression. The diversity within these movements highlights the challenges in characterising Egyptian Islam as a monolithic entity. Some groups focus on social service provision and community engagement, while others maintain a more overt political agenda. The state's response varies depending on the perceived threat level of each group, ranging from tolerance to outright suppression. This uneven application of state control generates further complexity and contributes to the inherent instability within the political system. The very act of trying to regulate religious expression creates a dynamic where the line between legitimate religious expression and political dissent becomes increasingly blurred.

The state's regulatory measures have profoundly impacted freedom of expression and religious practice in Egypt. While the Egyptian constitution guarantees freedom of religion, this freedom is subject to various restrictions and interpretations. The government's control over religious institutions, coupled with its crackdown on perceived threats to national security, has created an environment in which expressing religious views that differ from those of the state can lead to persecution. This has resulted in self-censorship, with many individuals and groups refraining from expressing dissenting religious or political views to avoid potential repercussions. The chilling effect of these restrictions is palpable, and it undermines the potential for open and inclusive political participation. This is particularly true for individuals and groups who identify with less mainstream religious interpretations or hold politically critical views.

The state's efforts to control religious discourse extend beyond the institutional level and into the digital realm. The government actively monitors online content, censoring material that it deems offensive or subversive. This online surveillance significantly impacts freedom of expression, preventing alternative religious perspectives from reaching a wider audience. Initially seen as a space for free expression, the digital realm has become increasingly restricted, reflecting the government's desire to maintain its grip on the flow of information and ideas. This comprehensive approach, which encompasses both physical and virtual spaces, showcases the state's determination to control the narrative surrounding religion in Egypt.

The impact of these state policies on women's participation in religious life and politics is also noteworthy. While some religious interpretations emphasise women's contributions within specific spheres of religious life, state policies often inadvertently marginalise women further. The suppression of religious movements and the imposition of strict control over religious institutions usually limit women's already constrained opportunities for religious leadership and political participation within religious frameworks. This intersection of gender and religious identity further compounds the challenges women face seeking to engage meaningfully in Egyptian political life. The absence of significant female representation in leadership positions within religious institutions, as well as the limited involvement of women in official religious discourse, highlights the extent to which state policies inadvertently reinforce patriarchal structures within religious contexts.

In conclusion, the relationship between religious identity and political participation in Egypt remains profoundly complex and deeply intertwined with the state's ongoing efforts to maintain political control. The state's relationship with Al-Azhar, the suppression of the Muslim Brotherhood, the regulation of religious discourse, and the restrictions on freedom of expression all contribute to a situation where religious identity is closely monitored and managed. While the state aims to maintain stability and prevent extremism, the resulting environment often suppresses genuine religious expression and limits the possibilities for inclusive political participation. The long-term consequences of these state-led measures remain uncertain. Still, their immediate impact is a constrained political space where religious identity is fraught with potential risks and limitations for political engagement. The future of Egypt's political landscape will depend, in part, on finding a more balanced approach that respects religious freedom while addressing legitimate security concerns.

Foreign Policy and Regional Roles Balancing Regional Alliances

Egypt's foreign policy is a complex tapestry woven with threads of pragmatism, self-interest, and a persistent need to balance its regional alliances amidst a volatile geopolitical landscape. Its approach reflects a long history of navigating competing power dynamics, from its colonial past to its current strategic positioning within the Middle East and Africa. Maintaining stability at home necessitates a delicate dance in foreign affairs, carefully calibrating relations with regional and international actors. Internal political realities further complicate this intricate balancing act, where domestic stability often dictates foreign policy choices and vice versa.

A cornerstone of Egypt's foreign policy has been its relationship with the United States. While the relationship has experienced fluctuations over the decades, largely dependent on the prevailing political climate in both countries, the US remains a crucial strategic partner for

Egypt. This relationship is underpinned by significant military aid, a cornerstone of Egypt's defence capabilities and a key element in its regional influence. This assistance, however, comes with caveats, often involving expectations of adherence to certain democratic principles and human rights standards, creating inherent tension between Cairo's strategic needs and Washington's diplomatic pressures. In recent years, we have witnessed a pragmatic alignment, with both countries focusing on counterterrorism efforts and regional stability, despite ongoing concerns regarding human rights. However, the military aid remains a crucial factor shaping Egypt's strategic decisions, influencing its regional posture and approach towards potentially contentious issues.

Conversely, Egypt has cultivated increasingly strong ties with Russia. This rapprochement represents a significant shift in its foreign policy, signifying a diversification of strategic partnerships and a reduced reliance on Western support. The relationship with Russia has been particularly marked by significant arms deals, bolstering Egypt's military capabilities and offering the US an alternative source of military technology. This deepening collaboration has also extended into economic and technological spheres, enhancing Egypt's economic diversification and strategic autonomy. The growing Russian influence has implications for Egypt's regional posture, allowing it to pursue independent policies without being entirely beholden to Western interests or pressures. This strategic pivot has implications for regional dynamics, creating a more complex interplay of power and interest.

Egypt's relationships with Arab neighbours are equally crucial, reflecting a complex mix of cooperation and competition. Relations with Saudi Arabia, a significant economic and political player in the region, are characterised by a blend of strategic collaboration and competition. While both countries share a common interest in regional stability and counterterrorism, competition for regional influence and differing perspectives on specific regional issues, such as the situation in Yemen, have created areas of friction. Economic ties between the two countries are substantial, with Saudi Arabia providing significant financial support to Egypt, but these ties are always interwoven with political considerations and power dynamics.

The relationship with other key Arab players also varies. Relations with the UAE have been powerful in recent years, with increasing levels of cooperation in economic, security and political spheres. Meanwhile, international regional dynamics and internal political changes have impacted relations with neighbours. The complexities and shifts in relationships among the Arab countries affect Egypt's strategies for maintaining stability in its surrounding region.

The evolving role of Egypt within regional organisations further shapes its foreign policy. Egypt's membership in the Arab League reflects its commitment to Arab unity and cooperation, even if the organisation's effectiveness is often debated. The Arab League's influence on Egypt's foreign policy is demonstrable on issues of mutual interest, although Egypt's independent pursuit of national interests usually takes precedence. The League's capacity to provide significant geopolitical leverage to Egypt is limited, but its symbolic importance and role in shaping regional perceptions remain substantial. Egypt's role in the African Union is also noteworthy, reflecting its aspiration to be a regional leader on the African continent. Its engagement with African countries reflects a strategic interest in expanding economic and political ties and leveraging its historical ties and influence on the continent. This continental focus allows Egypt to position itself as a major player beyond the confines of the Middle East, significantly expanding its geopolitical options and reducing over-reliance on Middle Eastern alliances.

Egypt's engagement with international organisations, particularly the United Nations, has also been significant. Its participation in UN peacekeeping missions and its active role in multilateral forums demonstrate its commitment to international cooperation and its desire to project a more globally positive image. However, its own human rights record often attracts criticism. This international visibility enables Egypt to maintain a powerful voice in global affairs, furthering its influence in international bodies while attempting to minimise potential negative fallout from internal human rights challenges.

Furthermore, the interplay between Egypt's internal politics and foreign policy is crucial. The domestic political climate significantly influences foreign policy choices. For example, the government's focus on domestic security has directly impacted its foreign policy priorities, increasing cooperation with countries with similar security concerns.

Conversely, the success or failure of foreign policy initiatives can have significant ramifications for domestic stability. For instance, failures in managing regional crises or diplomatic setbacks might amplify domestic grievances and instability. This intricate relationship indicates that Egypt's internal political priorities are often expressed, and even pursued, through foreign policy initiatives.

The Sisi administration's emphasis on economic development has also impacted foreign policy, leading to increased economic partnerships with countries that can provide investment and technology transfer. China is a particularly prominent example. This reflects a calculated strategy to mitigate economic challenges and bolster Egypt's long-term financial prospects. Economic considerations are increasingly being factored into foreign policy decisions, indicating a shift towards a more economically driven diplomatic strategy.

In conclusion, Egypt's foreign policy is dynamic and evolving, reflecting a complex interplay between regional alliances, international partnerships, and internal political realities. Its efforts to balance these competing demands demonstrate a pragmatic approach to safeguarding national interests, promoting regional stability, and enhancing its global standing. While the pursuit of stability at home remains a central driver of foreign policy choices, the constant recalibration of alliances and partnerships reflects the fluid and ever-changing nature of the geopolitical landscape in which Egypt operates. The continuing challenges, including economic pressures, regional conflicts, and internal political dynamics, underscore the complexity of navigating this intricate environment. The success of Egypt's foreign policy will ultimately depend on its ability to effectively balance these competing demands and adapt to the evolving dynamics of the global and regional political landscape.

Military Modernization and National Security Safeguarding National Interests

Egypt's military, a historically significant institution deeply interwoven with the nation's political fabric, has undergone a substantial modernisation process in recent decades. This modernisation is not merely upgrading equipment but a strategic recalibration of Egypt's national security priorities within a volatile regional context. The acquisition of advanced weaponry, the expansion of military capabilities, and the military's evolving role in domestic politics all contribute to a complex picture of Egypt's security posture. Understanding this transformation requires analysing the interplay between Egypt's national security concerns, economic capabilities, and evolving relationships with global powers.

A multifaceted set of security threats fuels the Egyptian military's modernisation drive. The rise of non-state actors, particularly extremist groups operating within the Sinai Peninsula and across the broader region, presents a persistent challenge. These groups, often benefiting from porous borders and the instability of neighbouring states, pose a direct threat to Egypt's territorial integrity and internal security. Counterterrorism operations, usually involving extensive military deployments and sophisticated weaponry, demand significant investment in advanced technology and training. This necessitates continuously upgrading equipment, including advanced surveillance systems, unmanned aerial vehicles (UAVs), and precision-guided munitions, to combat these evolving threats effectively.

Beyond counterterrorism, regional instability is a major driver of Egypt's military modernisation. The ongoing conflicts in Libya, Syria, and Yemen have created a volatile environment with spillover effects impacting Egypt's national security. The influx of refugees, the potential for cross-border incursions, and the threat of regional power struggles all necessitate a robust military capable of safeguarding Egypt's borders and protecting its national interests. The modernisation effort, therefore, is not solely focused on internal security; it extends to enhancing Egypt's ability to project power and influence in the region, deterring potential aggressors and safeguarding its strategic interests.

Egypt's military modernisation also reflects a desire to maintain its position as a regional power. While the country's economic woes pose constraints, the military's acquisition of advanced weaponry from various international partners underscores its determination to maintain a credible military deterrent. This ambition is not simply about maintaining a balance of power; it is intrinsically linked to Egypt's regional leadership aspirations and its pursuit of influence within international organisations. A modernised military enhances Egypt's bargaining power in regional negotiations, allows for greater participation in peacekeeping missions, and solidifies its role as a key player in resolving regional disputes.

The source of military equipment is a crucial aspect of this modernisation. Historically reliant on the United States for military aid, Egypt has increasingly diversified its sources of arms procurement. This diversification is driven by a desire to reduce dependence on any single supplier, enhance its strategic autonomy, and access a broader range of advanced technologies. Russia, in particular, has emerged as a significant supplier of advanced weaponry, including fighter jets and air defence systems. This shift towards Russia reflects a complex strategic calculation, balancing the benefits of diversified supply lines with the potential implications for Egypt's relationships with other global powers.

The economic dimensions of Egypt's military modernisation are equally significant. The substantial allocation of resources to the military, often a considerable portion of the national budget, necessitates careful economic planning and resource allocation. While precise figures are frequently debated, the military's budget reflects its importance in the government's strategic priorities. This substantial investment presents a trade-off between military spending and social development needs, prompting ongoing debates regarding economic priorities and the allocation of limited resources. This balancing act requires navigating the intricate interplay between national security needs and the demands of socio-economic development. Economic constraints frequently force the government to prioritise procurement projects and modernisation initiatives carefully, focusing on areas that offer the highest return on investment to enhance national security.

The military's influence on political decision-making is a further crucial aspect. The Egyptian army has historically played a significant role in the country's political life, wielding considerable influence beyond its traditional security responsibilities. This influence extends to domestic policy, economic planning, and even foreign policy decisions. While the degree of military involvement in politics is a subject of ongoing debate and varies over time, the military's capacity to influence national policies remains undeniable. This complex relationship necessitates understanding the dynamics of power-sharing, the influence of military leaders on key decisions, and the potential impact on political stability and democratic development.

The strategic implications of Egypt's military modernisation are far-reaching and complex. While enhancing Egypt's ability to protect its national interests, it also has implications for regional stability. The acquisition of advanced weaponry could potentially escalate regional tensions, prompting arms races and heightening the risks of conflict. Therefore, Egypt's efforts to balance its military modernisation with diplomatic initiatives to de-escalate tensions are crucial for ensuring regional peace and stability. This is particularly relevant given Egypt's significant role in regional power dynamics.

Moreover, Egypt's military modernisation impacts its relationship with global powers. The diversification of its military suppliers has altered its strategic alliances, reducing reliance on traditional partners and fostering new partnerships with countries such as Russia. This has implications for global power dynamics and the broader geopolitical landscape in the Middle East. This necessitates navigating a complex web of alliances and managing potential frictions with established partners while building new strategic relationships.

In conclusion, Egypt's military modernisation is a complex process driven by national security concerns, regional instability, and domestic politics. The acquisition of advanced weaponry, the diversification of arms suppliers, and the military's influence on political decision-making all contribute to a transformative shift in Egypt's security posture. While enhancing Egypt's ability to protect its national interests, this modernisation effort also carries significant regional and global implications. It requires careful navigation of complex power dynamics and balancing military preparedness and diplomatic engagement. The long-term success of Egypt's military modernisation strategy will depend on its ability to effectively manage these challenges and ensure that its military capabilities are used responsibly to foster regional stability and promote its long-term national interests.

Integrating modernisation with effective diplomatic strategies is critical in ensuring that increased military capabilities do not inadvertently destabilise the region, a delicate balancing act crucial for Egypt's future security and prosperity. Continued monitoring and analysis of Egypt's military spending and its deployment of resources will be essential in gauging the ultimate success of this complex undertaking.

Chapter 3
Türkiye: Balancing Domestic Politics and Regional Ambitions

Erdogans Legacy Consolidating Power and Redefining Turkish Identity

Recep Tayyip Erdoğan's rise to power and subsequent consolidation of authority have profoundly reshaped Türkiye's political landscape and its role in the international arena. His tenure, marked by a blend of authoritarian tendencies and populist appeal, has redefined Turkish identity, foreign policy, and the very fabric of Turkish society. Understanding Erdoğan's legacy requires examining the intricate interplay of domestic politics and regional ambitions, a complex dance that has profoundly impacted Türkiye's trajectory in the 21st century.

Erdoğan's initial ascent to the premiership in 2003, riding a wave of popular support, presented a departure from Türkiye's traditionally secular political establishment. His Justice and Development Party (AKP), with its roots in Islamist politics, promised a more inclusive and socially conservative agenda, resonating deeply with a significant portion of the Turkish electorate. Early years saw considerable economic growth and improvements in infrastructure, bolstering his popularity and the AKP's electoral dominance. However, this period also witnessed the erosion of secular traditions and a gradual centralisation of power around Erdoğan.

The gradual erosion of checks and balances within the Turkish political system was a hallmark of Erdoğan's consolidation of power. While initially working within the existing constitutional framework, his government systematically weakened opposition parties, curtailed media freedom, and neutralised judicial independence. The 2016 coup attempt, whether genuinely spontaneous or orchestrated as some believe, provided a pretext for further crackdowns on dissent. The subsequent purges within the military, judiciary, and civil service significantly diminished the potential for any meaningful challenge to his rule. Thousands were arrested, dismissed from their jobs, or forced into exile, creating a climate of fear and silencing critical voices.

The redefinition of Turkish identity under Erdoğan has been a central component of his political project. He has actively promoted a vision of a neo-Ottoman Türkiye, emphasising the country's historical legacy and seeking a more assertive role in the region. This has manifested in increased involvement in regional conflicts, often prioritising Turkish interests over diplomatic consensus. The promotion of a more conservative, religiously infused social order has further characterised this redefinition of identity, impacting the country's social fabric and its relationships with minority communities. Critics argue this has led to increased polarisation and a decline in religious and ethnic tolerance.

Both ambition and unpredictability have marked Erdoğan's foreign policy. His pursuit of a more assertive regional role has led to interventions in Syria, Libya, and other conflicts, often with mixed results and contributing to regional instability. Türkiye's increasingly strained relations with the European Union, primarily from human rights concerns and disagreements over immigration policy, highlight a shift away from traditional Western alliances. Pursuing closer ties with Russia and other non-Western powers underscores a willingness to challenge the established international order. The complex relationship with the United States, marked by periods of cooperation and intense friction, further reflects the intricacies of Türkiye's foreign policy maneuvering. This complex web of alliances and rivalries reflects a deliberate strategy of strategic autonomy and exposes Türkiye to significant geopolitical risks.

The economic policies under Erdoğan's rule have been considerably debated. While the early years witnessed impressive economic growth, recent years have seen a decline in economic stability, marked by high inflation and currency fluctuations. Critics argue that Erdoğan's preference for state intervention and control over economic decision-making has undermined market mechanisms and led to economic vulnerability. The government's emphasis on infrastructure projects, while enhancing certain aspects of the country's infrastructure, has been criticised for being unsustainable and inefficient in resource allocation.

Moreover, the government's response to economic challenges has been frequently inconsistent, further eroding investor confidence. The long-term sustainability of Türkiye's economic model under Erdoğan's leadership remains a central question.

Türkiye's human rights record under Erdoğan has deteriorated significantly. The crackdown on dissent following the 2016 coup attempt led to mass arrests, imprisonment of journalists and opposition figures, and significant restrictions on freedom of speech and expression. The judiciary's independence has been severely compromised, and due process protections have been increasingly undermined. These developments have drawn international condemnation, affecting Türkiye's relationship with international organisations and Western governments. The ongoing restrictions on Kurdish rights, along with the persecution of other minority groups, further contribute to human rights concerns. The lack of transparency and accountability in the justice system continues to be a significant concern, raising serious questions about the rule of law in the country.

The interplay between the ruling AKP, the opposition forces, and the military continues to shape Türkiye's political landscape. The AKP's dominance has been maintained mainly through electoral success, skillfully leveraging nationalist sentiment and populist appeals. However, the opposition continues to struggle to coalesce around a unified agenda, hindering their ability to challenge the AKP's hold on power. Despite being significantly weakened by the post-coup purges, the military remains a powerful institution, although its influence on political decision-making is considerably diminished compared to previous eras. The continuing tension between the government and sections of the military highlights the fragility of Türkiye's internal security situation.

Erdoğan's legacy will be complex and multifaceted. His supporters point to economic growth, infrastructural improvements, and a more assertive Turkish role on the global stage. However, critics emphasise the erosion of democratic norms, the suppression of dissent, and the deterioration of human rights. His emphasis on a revised, more religiously infused national identity has produced deep divisions within Turkish society. The long-term consequences of his policies, including the impact on the economy and Türkiye's geopolitical position, are yet to unfold fully. The extent to which Türkiye can sustain its regional ambitions while simultaneously navigating the challenges posed by internal divisions and strained international relations will fundamentally shape Erdoğan's lasting impact. The legacy of his rule will be debated for decades to come, and its true implications will likely be felt for generations.

The future of Turkish politics will likely depend on the ability of the opposition to challenge the AKP's dominance effectively. The current political climate, characterised by deep divisions and polarisation, hinders the creation of broad-based alliances capable of forming a credible alternative. The ongoing debate over Türkiye's identity, the balance between secular and religious influences, and the role of minorities in national life will continue to shape the country's political trajectory. The challenges faced by Türkiye in the years to come, including economic instability, regional conflicts, and internal political tensions, will demand deft leadership and strategic decision-making. The success of Türkiye in navigating these challenges will be a key determinant of its future stability and prosperity. The country's relations with the West, including its membership aspirations within organisations like the EU, will continue to be influenced by the extent to which human rights and democratic norms are upheld. The international community will be key in encouraging reforms that foster democratic values and address human rights concerns. This process will significantly impact Türkiye's ongoing evolution. The ongoing evolution of Türkiye's role in regional conflicts and its relationship with major global powers will likewise influence its long-term trajectory. The future remains uncertain, but its contours will be defined by the interplay of internal political dynamics, economic realities, and its evolving place in the complex geopolitical landscape of the 21st century.

Economic Transformation and Development Challenges Navigating Global Markets

Türkiye's economic trajectory under Erdoğan's leadership presents a complex picture, marked by periods of impressive growth juxtaposed with significant vulnerabilities. While the early years of the AKP's rule witnessed considerable economic expansion, fueled by both domestic consumption and foreign investment, the model's sustainability has been increasingly questioned in recent years. The economy's dependence on specific sectors, coupled with fluctuating global economic conditions and domestic policy choices, has created an environment of financial instability.

A key feature of the Turkish economy is its significant reliance on tourism. The influx of foreign tourists contributes substantially to the country's GDP, providing employment and revenue. However, this dependence creates inherent vulnerability. Global events, such as economic downturns or geopolitical instability in regions popular with tourists, can significantly impact tourism revenues, causing ripples throughout the economy. The COVID-19 pandemic serves as a stark example, with the sharp decline in international travel causing a considerable blow to Türkiye's tourism sector and triggering a broader economic downturn. Diversifying the economy away from such over-reliance on tourism remains a crucial challenge for Türkiye.

The manufacturing sector plays a vital role in the Turkish economy, employing a significant portion of the workforce and contributing significantly to exports. However, the industry faces competitiveness, innovation, and technological advancement challenges. While Türkiye has made progress in specific manufacturing sub-sectors, it often lags behind other developed and emerging economies regarding technological sophistication and value-added production. The government's efforts to promote industrial development have been met with mixed success, with concerns remaining about the efficiency of resource allocation and the effectiveness of industrial policies. Furthermore, the global competition in manufacturing continues to intensify, presenting further challenges for Turkish producers. The need for technological upgrades and innovation to maintain international competitiveness is critical for Türkiye's manufacturing sector.

Türkiye's trade relations are multifaceted, reflecting its strategic location at the crossroads of Europe and Asia. The country maintains significant trade links with the European Union, its largest trading partner. However, the relationship has been strained in recent years, due to political disagreements and concerns over human rights and democratic backsliding. Türkiye also trades substantially with countries in the Middle East, Asia, and Africa. Pursuing closer economic ties with countries such as Russia and China signifies a shift in Türkiye's trade strategy, aiming to reduce its dependence on Western markets and diversify its trade partners. However, this diversification presents challenges, as different markets have different requirements and demand different approaches. Balancing these multiple trade relationships requires skilful diplomacy and effective economic management.

The impact of global economic trends on Türkiye's economy is considerable. Global economic shocks, such as the 2008 financial crisis or the recent disruptions caused by the war in Ukraine, can significantly affect Türkiye's economy, given its relatively open economic structure. Fluctuations in global commodity prices, particularly energy prices, can also severely impact Türkiye's economic performance. The country's large current account deficit makes it particularly vulnerable to external economic shocks. Managing these external vulnerabilities and mitigating the impact of global economic fluctuations is a critical task for Turkish policymakers.

Specific economic policies implemented under Erdoğan's leadership have significantly affected various segments of Turkish society. The government's emphasis on infrastructure projects, while contributing to employment and boosting specific sectors, has also been criticised for its high cost and questionable economic viability in some instances. While intended to stimulate growth, the focus on state intervention and government control over the economy has also been associated with concerns about transparency, efficiency, and the distortion of market mechanisms. These policies have had varying impacts across different population segments, exacerbating existing inequalities in some cases. The long-term consequences of these economic policies on income distribution, social welfare, and financial stability remain to be fully assessed.

The Turkish government's handling of inflation has been another point of concern. High and persistent inflation has eroded purchasing power, particularly impacting low-income households. The government's response to inflation has often been inconsistent, undermining investor confidence and causing currency fluctuations. Despite high inflation, the government's reliance on interest rate cuts contradicts conventional economic wisdom and has contributed to instability. This divergence from orthodox economic policy has raised concerns among international financial institutions and investors.

Despite its importance in providing employment and food security, the agricultural sector faces challenges in modernisation, productivity, and market access. While efforts have been made to support the farm sector, there is room for significant improvement in efficiency, technology adoption, and market integration. The impact of climate change on agricultural yields also represents a serious concern that demands immediate and effective measures.

The energy sector is another crucial area requiring careful management. Türkiye's reliance on energy imports makes it vulnerable to global price fluctuations. Developing domestic energy resources and diversifying energy sources are vital for enhancing the country's energy security and mitigating the economic risks associated with energy dependence. Investing in renewable energy and promoting energy efficiency are essential aspects of this strategy.

In addition to these economic challenges, corruption and governance issues remain significant obstacles to Türkiye's economic progress. Transparency and accountability in public finance and the rule of law are essential for fostering a climate conducive to investment and economic growth. Strengthening institutions and enhancing governance are crucial for mitigating the adverse effects of corruption and improving the overall investment climate.

In conclusion, Türkiye's economic transformation and development present a mixed record. While periods of strong growth have been witnessed, vulnerabilities remain. The country's dependence on specific sectors, exposure to global economic shocks, and domestic policy choices have contributed to economic instability. Addressing the challenges of diversification, technological innovation, fiscal sustainability, inflation management, and governance remains crucial for ensuring Türkiye's long-term economic prosperity and equitable growth. The choices made regarding economic policy will shape the nation's economic trajectory and future social and political landscape. Navigating the global market effectively requires a strategic approach that balances national interests with the demands of a globalised economy, while addressing social inequalities and protecting the environment. The long-term sustainability of Türkiye's economic model will depend on the ability of its leaders to address these multifaceted challenges effectively and efficiently.

Religious Identity and Secularism A Contested Terrain

The narrative of modern Türkiye is inextricably intertwined with the complex and often contested relationship between religious identity and secularism. Kemal Atatürk's revolutionary project, following the collapse of the Ottoman Empire, aimed to forge a distinctly modern, secular Turkish state, sharply contrasting with its religiously infused predecessor. This involved sweeping reforms dismantling the traditional religious establishment, replacing Islamic law with a secular legal code, and promoting a secularised public sphere. The Latin alphabet replaced the Arabic script, and religious education was significantly curtailed in favour of a Westernised curriculum. While Atatürk's vision aimed to create a cohesive national identity transcending religious differences, the legacy of this secularising project remains a subject of ongoing debate and political maneuvering.

The post-Atatürk era witnessed a gradual, albeit often suppressed, resurgence of religious influence in public life. While the officially secular framework remained in place, the state's strict control over religious expression gradually loosened, allowing for greater religious freedom, although unevenly distributed across different religious communities. The military, long considered the guardian of secularism, frequently intervened in politics, often invoking the defence of secular principles to justify coups and crackdowns on perceived threats to the secular order. This pattern solidified the perception of secularism as a tool for maintaining political power, rather than a principle protecting individual religious freedom.

The rise of the Justice and Development Party (AKP) under Recep Tayyip Erdoğan marked a significant turning point in Türkiye's relationship with religion and secularism. The AKP, rooted in a moderate Islamist ideology, cleverly navigated the delicate balance between appealing to religiously conservative segments of the population and maintaining a facade of adherence to the secular constitution. Their approach involved incremental changes, subtly shifting the boundaries of religious expression in public spaces while avoiding confrontation with the entrenched secular establishment. This strategy resonated deeply with many Turkish citizens who felt alienated by the officially enforced secularism of the previous era. The AKP's triumphant electoral victories demonstrated the increasing political influence of religiously conservative voters.

The AKP's policies have been characterised by a gradual, albeit contested, expansion of the role of religion in public life. The lifting of restrictions on wearing the headscarf in public institutions, for example, is seen by many as a symbolic victory for religious conservatives. The increased funding for religious education and institutions and the promotion of religious figures in public discourse represent a shift away from the strict separation of religion and state characteristic of Atatürk's era. However, it's crucial to understand that this expansion of religious influence is not uniformly applied. While some religious groups have seen increased recognition and support, others, particularly Alevis and other minority religious communities, have often found themselves marginalised and their religious practices subject to state restrictions.

The government's policies regarding religious freedom have also been a source of significant controversy and debate. While the constitution guarantees freedom of religion, its implementation has been uneven. Claims of religious discrimination and restrictions on religious expression persist, particularly targeting minority groups. While the AKP government has made efforts to engage with different religious communities, concerns remain regarding the consistent application of religious freedoms and the protection of religious minorities' rights. The state's control over the appointment of religious leaders within the Directorate of Religious Affairs (Diyanet) raises questions about religious autonomy and freedom from government interference. The Diyanet's extensive reach and influence, particularly in education and public discourse, have also led to concerns regarding the promotion of a particular interpretation of Islam, often criticised as overly conservative.

The relationship between the state and specific religious communities is complex and multifaceted. The Sunni Muslim majority, while generally benefiting from the AKP's policies, experiences internal divisions regarding the appropriate balance between religion and state. The Alevi community, often seen as a minority within the broader Muslim community in Türkiye, faces persistent challenges in securing complete religious freedom and recognition of their distinct religious traditions. The government's interactions with this community have been marked by both periods of cooperation and tension, reflecting the ongoing struggle to reconcile religious diversity within a framework often perceived as favouring a particular interpretation of Islam. Other religious minorities, such as Christians, Jews, and Yazidis, also face unique challenges in balancing their religious practices within the broader socio-political context.

Legislative measures impacting religious institutions highlight the ongoing tension between secularism and religious influence. While some legislation has aimed to foster greater religious freedom, other laws have been criticised for restricting religious expression and infringing upon the autonomy of religious organisations. The legal framework governing the establishment and functioning of religious institutions has been subject to ongoing review and modification, reflecting the constantly evolving dynamic between the state and religious communities. The legal battles and ongoing debates surrounding these legislative measures often highlight the deep divisions within Turkish society regarding the appropriate relationship between the state and religious affairs.

The interplay between secularism and Islamism in Türkiye is not simply a top-down phenomenon orchestrated solely by government policies. It is a dynamic interaction shaped by many factors, including societal attitudes, evolving religious practices, and the changing political landscape. The ongoing debates surrounding religious freedom, the role of the Diyanet, and the legal framework governing religious institutions reflect the multifaceted and deeply rooted nature of this complex relationship. The struggle to reconcile the legacy of Atatürk's secularising project with the growing influence of religious conservatives continues to shape Turkish politics and social life. Whether Türkiye can find a sustainable model that accommodates its secular heritage and the evolving religious landscape, fostering inclusivity and ensuring genuine religious freedom for all its citizens, this intricate balancing act will undoubtedly continue to define Türkiye's trajectory in the future.

Furthermore, the international community's perception of Türkiye's human rights record and its treatment of minority religious groups will have implications for its foreign relations and geopolitical standing. The ongoing dialogue surrounding these critical issues will be essential in shaping Türkiye's future domestically and internationally.

Dr. Shaikh Mohammad Shahriyar Wahab

The challenge lies in fostering a society where religious diversity is not just tolerated but celebrated, and where individual religious freedom is genuinely protected, regardless of religious affiliation. Achieving this balance requires continuous dialogue, mutual understanding, and a commitment to democratic principles.

Foreign Policy and Regional Influence A Multifaceted Approach

Türkiye's assertive foreign policy under the Justice and Development Party (AKP) represents a significant departure from its previous, more cautious approach to international relations. This shift reflects domestic political imperatives and a broader ambition to reassert Türkiye's regional and global influence. The country's actions demonstrate a multifaceted approach, balancing cooperation with confrontation, depending on the context and national interests.

One of the most striking aspects of Türkiye's foreign policy is its increasing engagement in regional conflicts. The Syrian civil war provides a compelling case study. Initially, Türkiye supported the Syrian opposition, providing refuge for Syrian refugees and offering logistical and even military support to anti-Assad factions. This intervention stemmed from concerns about the potential spillover of the conflict into Türkiye, the rise of extremist groups like

ISIS within Syria, and Türkiye's long-standing historical and strategic interests in the region, particularly concerning the Kurdish population along its southern border. However, Türkiye's approach has evolved significantly, reflecting the shifting dynamics and its changing strategic priorities. The changing relationship with Russia and the rise of Kurdish autonomy within Syria have led Türkiye to engage in military operations within Syria, sometimes clashing with other actors, including Kurdish militias supported by the United States. This underscores the complexity and fluidity of Türkiye's foreign policy choices, driven by a combination of security concerns, geopolitical ambitions, and domestic political pressures.

The Libyan conflict serves as another example of Türkiye's active regional engagement. Türkiye's support for the internationally recognised Government of National Accord (GNA) in Tripoli was based on the strategic calculation that supporting a moderate government in Libya, even if faltering and under attack, better served its interests than allowing the potential emergence of a more radical or regional rival-backed administration. This involvement extended to providing military assistance and training to GNA forces, which involved deploying military personnel and equipment. The implications for the regional balance of power were profound, and particularly important for Türkiye's influence in the Eastern Mediterranean. The strategic impact of Türkiye's role in Libya's civil war extends beyond the immediate geopolitical environment, encompassing the regional control of maritime routes and natural resources and the influence on the broader political landscape of North Africa.

Türkiye's relations with the European Union (EU) are another key aspect of its foreign policy. While Türkiye has long aspired to EU membership, this process has been fraught with difficulties and marked by periods of cooperation and tension. Concerns about human rights, the rule of law, and press freedom in Türkiye have fueled criticism from the EU, slowing down and halting the progress of accession negotiations. The cyclical nature of the relationship shows how Türkiye's domestic political environment and the EU's internal dynamics frequently impact their diplomatic and economic engagements. This tension extends to disputes over the status of Cyprus and the Aegean Sea, where conflicting claims over maritime boundaries and energy resources have led to diplomatic standoffs and increased military activity. The EU's response to Türkiye's actions in these areas has often been divided and inconsistent, leading to criticism and engagement with the Turkish government. In effect, Türkiye leverages its strategic location and geopolitical influence to navigate this challenging relationship, sometimes employing a strategy that involves playing on the differing internal priorities within the EU.

Türkiye's relationship with Russia presents a complex and evolving dynamic. While there have been periods of cooperation, particularly in areas such as energy and defence, there have also been significant frictions, particularly over the Syrian civil war, the annexation of

Crimea, and disputes in the Black Sea region. Türkiye's willingness to strike deals with Russia, even in areas with significant disagreement with the West, exemplifies its capacity for strategic pragmatism. This reflects an effort to balance its foreign policy aspirations while navigating a complex and multifaceted relationship with a significant regional power. Despite US objections, Türkiye's acquisition of Russian S-400 missile defence systems is a prime example of this approach. This decision highlighted Türkiye's determination to pursue its national security interests, even at the expense of straining its relationship with NATO allies. The balancing act between close ties to NATO and a pragmatic relationship with Russia underscores Türkiye's challenges and choices in managing its foreign policy.

Türkiye's relationships with other regional players, such as Iran, Israel, and the Arab states, also showcase its capacity for multifaceted engagement. A combination of historical ties, strategic interests, and domestic political considerations often shapes its approach. For instance, the relationship with Iran, while complex and usually fraught with tension, has also been marked by periods of cooperation, particularly about regional security issues. This cooperation often hinges on managing competing national interests and finding common ground on critical areas of convergence, such as regional stability and counter-terrorism efforts against extremist groups. With Israel, relations have fluctuated dramatically, reflecting the complexities of regional dynamics and internal domestic political debates. Türkiye's relationship with several Arab states presents a similar spectrum, frequently moving between engagement and distancing depending on the particular political and strategic landscape.

The economic dimension of Türkiye's foreign policy is also critical. Türkiye has actively pursued trade agreements and economic partnerships with numerous countries, aiming to diversify its economic ties and reduce dependence on any single partner. This strategy reflects a recognition of the country's growing economic strength and its ambition to play a larger role in the global economy. This economic focus is not just about material gains; it's a strategic tool used to influence political relations and assert Türkiye's influence on a global stage, offering economic incentives or withdrawing support to achieve its diplomatic objectives. This highlights the interconnectivity of economic and political strategies in Türkiye's broader approach to international relations.

In conclusion, Türkiye's foreign policy under the AKP era is characterised by an assertive and multi-faceted approach, balancing cooperation and confrontation depending on strategic considerations and domestic political imperatives. This complex strategy reflects its engagement in regional conflicts, its relationship with the EU, its balancing act with Russia, and its interactions with other regional players. This approach has enhanced Türkiye's regional influence and generated considerable controversy, highlighting the challenges and complexities of navigating a rapidly changing geopolitical landscape. The future of Turkish foreign policy will depend on its ability to manage these complexities, balance competing interests, and adapt to ongoing shifts in the international system. The ongoing domestic debates within Türkiye surrounding these foreign policy initiatives also underscore the vital link between internal political currents and external policy, emphasising the need for a nuanced understanding of how domestic realities shape Türkiye's actions on the world stage. The success of Türkiye's foreign policy hinges on its ability to maintain a delicate balance between its domestic priorities and its broader regional and global ambitions.

Military Modernization and Regional Security Strategic Implications

Türkiye's pursuit of regional influence is inextricably linked to its military modernisation efforts. A significant portion of the country's budget is allocated to defence spending, reflecting the government's commitment to maintaining a robust and technologically advanced military force. This investment is driven by several factors, including the need to address internal security threats, manage its complex relationships with neighbouring countries, and project power within its sphere of influence. Modernisation has involved significant acquisitions of advanced weaponry and equipment, focusing on air power, naval capabilities, and ground forces. Türkiye's acquisition of advanced fighter jets, drones, and air defence systems has substantially enhanced its military capabilities. The indigenous development of military technology, particularly in unmanned aerial vehicles (UAVs), has given Türkiye a competitive edge in regional conflicts and broadened its export opportunities. The development and export of

Turkish-made drones have become a crucial aspect of the country's military and foreign policy, creating economic and strategic leverage on the global stage.

The impact of Türkiye's military modernisation on regional security is multifaceted and complex. Its enhanced capabilities have allowed it to play a more significant role in several regional conflicts, most notably in Syria, Libya, and the Nagorno-Karabakh conflict. In Syria, Türkiye's military intervention, primarily aimed at countering Kurdish forces and supporting Syrian opposition groups, has significantly shaped the battlefield dynamics. These actions, however, have also led to increased tensions with other regional and global actors, including the United States and Russia, raising concerns about escalating proxy conflicts and unintended consequences. The use of Turkish-made drones in these conflicts has further complicated the geopolitical landscape, adding a layer of technological asymmetry that has altered the dynamics of conventional warfare in the region.

The Libyan conflict provides another case study of Türkiye's evolving military role. Türkiye's military support for the Government of National Accord (GNA), in the face of challenges from the Libyan National Army (LNA), was a decisive factor in the outcome of the conflict. This support, involving the deployment of military personnel, equipment, and training, demonstrated Türkiye's willingness to employ hard power to pursue its strategic objectives in North Africa. The consequences of this intervention have been profound, shaping the political landscape of Libya and solidifying Türkiye's regional influence over critical maritime routes and energy resources. However, Türkiye's involvement has not been without controversy. Critics have raised concerns about the implications of foreign intervention on Libyan sovereignty and the potential for further destabilisation.

Türkiye's military involvement in the Nagorno-Karabakh conflict, supporting Azerbaijan, underscores its increasing regional assertiveness. This intervention, marked by the effective use of its technologically advanced military equipment, particularly drones, demonstrates Türkiye's commitment to supporting its allies and projecting its military capabilities beyond its immediate borders. The success in this conflict has raised concerns about the potential for further escalation of conflicts in the region, specifically the impact of Türkiye's increasingly active role in shaping the regional power balance. The strategic implications for the South Caucasus region are significant, potentially redefining regional alliances and increasing great power rivalry.

Türkiye's military modernisation implications for its relationship with NATO are complex. While a key member of the alliance, Türkiye's acquisition of the Russian S-400 missile defence system has strained its relations with the United States and other NATO members. This decision, driven by Türkiye's national security priorities, highlights the challenges of balancing its commitment to the alliance with its strategic interests. The ensuing sanctions imposed on Türkiye have underscored the limitations and potential costs of pursuing independent defence strategies while maintaining membership in a collective security framework.

The future of Türkiye's relationship with NATO will hinge on finding solutions that address the concerns of all member states while allowing Türkiye to maintain its security needs and strategic autonomy.

Beyond its regional engagements, Türkiye's military modernisation also has implications for its global relations. Its growing military capabilities have increased its influence in international organisations such as the Organisation of Islamic Cooperation (OIC) and the United Nations. However, Türkiye's assertive military posture has also provoked international criticism. Concerns regarding human rights abuses in its military operations and the potential for unintended escalations through military interventions have highlighted the complexities of balancing national security interests with international norms and global stability.

Furthermore, Türkiye's military modernisation efforts have significant economic implications. The substantial investment in defence spending diverts resources from other areas of the economy, potentially impacting social programs and economic development. However, the development and export of indigenous military technology have created new economic opportunities, contributing to growth in the defence industry and promoting Türkiye's export-led growth strategy. The inherent duality of these economic effects highlights the critical need for Türkiye to balance its investment in military capabilities with domestic economic and social needs.

The analysis of Türkiye's military modernisation necessitates consideration of the interplay between domestic politics and foreign policy. The government's commitment to military modernisation is closely linked to its domestic political agenda and strategic national identity. The AKP's emphasis on national strength and regional leadership is reflected in its military capabilities and assertive foreign policy investment. Internal political debates surrounding military spending and foreign policy decisions highlight the direct link between the domestic political environment and Türkiye's military engagement in regional affairs. Understanding this interconnectedness is crucial for comprehending the rationale behind Türkiye's military actions and their regional implications.

In conclusion, Türkiye's military modernisation significantly shapes regional security. Its enhanced capabilities have increased its ability to project power, influence the outcomes of regional conflicts, and assert its interests in international forums. However, this assertive military posture has also increased tensions with other regional and global actors, raising concerns about unintended consequences and the potential for escalating conflicts. The ongoing effects of Türkiye's actions require continuous monitoring, given the sensitivity of the geopolitical situation and the interconnected nature of regional stability. The intricate relationship between Türkiye's domestic politics and military modernisation emphasises its role's complex and dynamic nature in regional security. Further research is needed to analyse the long-term consequences of Türkiye's military modernisation on regional stability and its overall relationship with both regional and global actors. The evolving security landscape of the Middle East and the continuing complexities of Turkish foreign policy will require continuous evaluation of Türkiye's military modernisation strategy and its impact on regional stability.

Chapter 4
Pakistan: Balancing Internal Security and Geopolitical Pressures

Political Instability and Security Concerns A Persistent Challenge

Pakistan's journey since its inception has been punctuated by periods of both relative stability and profound instability. Understanding this fluctuating trajectory requires examining the intricate interplay of several factors: the powerful military establishment, the volatile nature of its domestic politics, and the persistent threat of extremist groups. The country's geopolitical location, straddling the volatile Afghanistan-Iran border and facing regional rivalries, further compounds its challenges.

The military's pervasive influence on Pakistani politics is undeniable. Since independence, the army has ruled the country for significant periods, intervening in civilian governments deemed weak or ineffective. This interventionist tradition has shaped the political landscape, creating a culture where military influence permeates even ostensibly civilian administrations. The allocation of a disproportionate share of the national budget to defence further underscores the military's prominence and ability to shape national priorities. The military's rationale for intervention often centres on maintaining national security, particularly in regional instability and the threat of internal conflict. However, the military's role has frequently been criticised for undermining democratic processes, suppressing dissent, and hindering the development of strong civilian institutions. This enduring tension between military dominance and the aspirations for democratic governance continues to be a defining feature of Pakistani politics.

The rise of religious extremism poses another significant challenge to Pakistan's stability. The country's history is intertwined with religious movements, some of which have evolved into violent extremist groups. The rise of these groups, fueled by various factors including socio-economic grievances, political marginalisation, and the influence of external actors, has led to an environment of insecurity and violence. The Pakistani state has struggled to effectively counter this threat, facing challenges in both military operations and in addressing the underlying socio-political factors contributing to extremism. This struggle has resulted in numerous terrorist attacks, targeting both civilian and military populations, and has destabilised regions within Pakistan. The interplay between the state's security apparatus and the extremist groups is a complex one, often marked by periods of intense conflict, uneasy truces, and accusations of tacit collaboration. The long-term consequences of this unresolved conflict continue to pose a significant threat to Pakistan's internal security and its broader regional relations.

The complex relationship between the state and various political factions further contributes to instability. Pakistan's political parties often operate within a highly competitive and sometimes adversarial environment. Coalition governments, formed due to the lack of single-party majorities, usually prove fragile and short-lived, resulting in frequent changes in leadership and policy. This dynamic is further complicated by the influence of robust familial and tribal networks, which can override institutional processes and contribute to political gridlock. The frequent accusations of corruption and lack of accountability within the political system have eroded public trust and fostered cynicism towards democratic institutions. This has created an environment where extremist narratives can gain traction, further exacerbating the existing instability.

The Balochistan conflict represents a prime example of Pakistan's internal security challenges. This province, rich in natural resources, has been the site of a long-running insurgency fueled by grievances related to underdevelopment, political marginalisation, and human rights abuses. Baloch nationalist groups have waged a protracted struggle for greater autonomy or even independence, engaging in armed conflict with the Pakistani state. The conflict has claimed numerous lives and hindered economic development in the region. The state's response to the insurgency has included military operations, leading to further human rights concerns and a cycle of violence. Resolving the Balochistan conflict requires addressing the underlying socio-economic and political grievances fueling the insurgency, a process that will require substantial political will and commitment to reconciliation.

External actors seeking to exploit the internal instability for their strategic goals further complicate the security situation. Pakistan's proximity to Afghanistan has made it particularly vulnerable to spillover effects from the ongoing conflict in that country. The porous border has allowed for the movement of militants and fighters, making it difficult to contain the threat of cross-border terrorism fully. Furthermore, regional geopolitical rivalries, particularly the intense competition between India and Pakistan, have destabilised the region. The continuing Kashmir dispute remains a significant source of tension between the two nuclear-armed neighbours, with periodic military escalations and an ongoing low-level conflict. This heightened tension creates an environment of insecurity for both countries' populations and draws in external actors, who may seek to destabilise the region for further purposes.

The economic challenges facing Pakistan also contribute to its political instability. The country faces persistent poverty, inequality, and a lack of sufficient investment in human capital. This economic precariousness creates fertile ground for resentment, social unrest, and the recruitment of individuals into extremist groups. The dependence on foreign aid and loans can also limit the state's policy options and create vulnerabilities to external influence. The fluctuations in the global economy and the volatility of commodity prices further add to the country's challenges. Addressing Pakistan's economic problems requires long-term structural reforms, focusing on sustainable economic growth, improved governance, and equitable distribution of resources. Without significant improvements in the financial sphere, the likelihood of political instability will remain high.

Pakistan's efforts to counter terrorism and extremism have involved both military operations and counter-terrorism strategies. However, the long-term success of these efforts depends on addressing the root causes of extremism, including poverty, lack of education, and political marginalisation. Developing strong democratic institutions, effective governance, and a focus on human rights are all essential to a lasting solution. Furthermore, improved regional cooperation and dialogue are crucial to addressing the external factors that contribute to instability. The challenge for Pakistan is to find a balance between maintaining national security, addressing its internal security threats, and fostering peaceful relations with its neighbours while promoting economic development. The ongoing complexities of Pakistan's internal and external security environment underscore the need for comprehensive, multi-faceted strategies focused on hard and soft power to address the deep-rooted problems contributing to its instability. The success of these strategies will require political will, a commitment to reform, and a focus on fostering inclusive and sustainable development that addresses the grievances of all segments of Pakistani society. The path toward lasting stability remains challenging but essential for Pakistan's future.

Economic Development and Poverty Alleviation Addressing Structural Issues

Pakistan's economic landscape is deeply intertwined with its political instability and security concerns. The country's persistent struggles with poverty, inequality, and a reliance on foreign aid significantly hinder its ability to achieve sustainable development and bolster national security. Addressing these structural economic issues is not merely an economic imperative but a crucial element of ensuring long-term stability and national resilience.

One of the most pressing challenges is widespread poverty. While Pakistan has made strides in reducing poverty rates in certain regions and among specific demographics, significant pockets of extreme poverty persist, particularly in rural areas and among marginalised communities. This poverty is not simply a matter of lacking financial resources; it manifests as limited access to education, healthcare, clean water, and sanitation. This, in turn, fuels a cycle of deprivation that is difficult to break. The lack of adequate access to education limits opportunities for upward mobility, perpetuates intergenerational poverty, and hinders the development of a skilled workforce necessary for economic diversification and growth. Similarly, poor healthcare outcomes, high infant and maternal mortality rates, and limited access to basic healthcare services place a heavy burden on families and communities, contributing to economic hardship.

The issue of inequality further complicates the economic picture. A significant wealth gap exists between the elite and the masses, with a disproportionate share of national wealth concentrated in the hands of a relatively small segment of the population. This vast disparity in wealth distribution undermines social cohesion, fosters resentment, and contributes to social unrest. The unequal access to resources and opportunities exacerbates existing inequalities, hindering inclusive growth and undermining the stability of society as a whole. Policies addressing inequality need to go beyond simply targeting poverty alleviation; they must address the systemic issues perpetuating this disparity, such as unequal access to land ownership, limited access to credit for small businesses, and discriminatory practices in the labour market.

Pakistan's reliance on foreign aid and loans has long been a source of economic vulnerability. While foreign assistance has played a role in supporting economic development initiatives, the country's dependence on external funding makes it susceptible to external pressures and fluctuations in global financial conditions. This dependence can also limit the government's policy autonomy, hindering the implementation of bold and necessary reforms. A shift toward sustainable and domestically driven economic growth is crucial to reducing this dependence and building long-term financial resilience.

The country's efforts to diversify its economy beyond its traditional reliance on agriculture and textiles have yielded mixed results. While the service sector has grown significantly, contributing substantially to the GDP, its growth has not been inclusive enough to absorb the growing labour force. Moreover, despite significant potential, the manufacturing sector remains underdeveloped, hampered by inefficient infrastructure, lack of technological access, and bureaucratic hurdles. Promoting a more dynamic and diversified manufacturing sector is essential for creating higher-paying jobs, reducing reliance on imports, and fostering sustainable economic growth.

Infrastructure development is another critical aspect of Pakistan's economic strategy. Investments in improving transportation networks, energy infrastructure, and communication systems are crucial for enhancing productivity, attracting foreign investment, and facilitating trade. The lack of adequate infrastructure, particularly in rural areas, significantly hinders economic activity and exacerbates regional disparities. Infrastructure improvement is not a mere economic issue; it is a significant factor in improving the quality of life for millions of Pakistanis, providing access to markets, healthcare, and educational opportunities.

Attracting foreign direct investment (FDI) is also a key component of Pakistan's economic development plan. However, persistent concerns about political instability, security risks, and bureaucratic inefficiencies deter potential investors. Improving the business environment, reducing corruption, and implementing transparent and predictable policies are essential to creating a more conducive environment for attracting FDI. The government's efforts to promote investment should focus on transparency, the rule of law, and ensuring a level playing field for domestic and foreign investors.

The effects of economic policies on various sectors of Pakistani society are multifaceted and complex. Agricultural policies, for example, directly impact rural livelihoods, while industrial policies shape urban employment opportunities. Trade policies affect the competitiveness of both domestic industries and export sectors. Social welfare programs, such as targeted subsidies and poverty alleviation initiatives, directly influence the living standards of vulnerable populations. Analysing the impacts of these policies requires considering their distributional effects across different socioeconomic groups and geographic regions, paying close attention to unintended consequences and ensuring equitable access to resources.

Specific economic policies enacted by the Pakistani government have had varied outcomes. Some policies have succeeded in certain areas, while others have fallen short of their intended goals. For example, initiatives promoting private sector growth have shown some success in expanding specific industries, but have often failed to address widespread unemployment and inequality. Similarly, measures to improve agricultural productivity have yielded some positive results, but have not been consistently effective in raising rural incomes and reducing rural poverty. A thorough evaluation of the successes and failures of past policies is essential for informing the design of future economic strategies.

Addressing Pakistan's economic challenges requires a comprehensive and multi-faceted approach. This approach should focus on sustainable and inclusive growth, improving governance, enhancing human capital, and reducing reliance on foreign aid. Structural reforms targeting poverty, inequality, and infrastructure development are crucial. These reforms must prioritise long-term solutions rather than short-term fixes and ensure equity across regions and socioeconomic groups. Additionally, fostering an environment conducive to private sector investment, promoting technological innovation, and strengthening regional trade ties are essential components of a long-term economic development strategy. Finally, fostering a strong sense of national unity and social cohesion will be critical to the success of any economic development endeavour. Without addressing these deeper, societal issues, the country will struggle to achieve sustainable and inclusive development, regardless of the economic policies implemented. Pakistan can hope to achieve lasting financial stability and prosperity through a comprehensive and sustained commitment to structural reform and inclusive growth, strengthening its national security and global standing.

Religious Identity and Societal Divisions A Fragmented Landscape

Pakistan's identity is profoundly shaped by its religious composition, creating a complex and often volatile social and political landscape. While Islam is the state religion, the country is home to a significant number of religious minorities, including Christians, Hindus, Sikhs, and others. The relationship between these groups and the state and the dynamics of the different religious communities significantly influence the nation's internal security and ability to navigate geopolitical pressures.

The constitution guarantees religious freedom, yet reality is often far more nuanced and challenging. Discrimination against religious minorities persists in various forms, including legal limitations, social stigma, and instances of targeted violence. While the government has enacted laws aimed at protecting religious minorities, their enforcement remains inconsistent, and loopholes often allow for discriminatory practices to continue. The lack of effective implementation is usually attributed to a combination of factors, including bureaucratic inertia, societal prejudices, and sometimes, the complicity of state actors. For instance, blasphemy laws, though intended to protect religious sentiments, have been frequently misused to target minorities, leading to extrajudicial killings and mob violence. These incidents not only violate the human rights of religious minorities but also undermine the rule of law and exacerbate societal divisions. Moreover, the lack of consistent and impartial investigation and prosecution of those who misuse blasphemy laws creates a climate of fear and insecurity for religious minorities.

The historical context is crucial to understanding the current situation. The partition of India in 1947, which led to the creation of Pakistan as a separate Muslim state, profoundly shaped the country's religious identity and the relationship between its various communities. The trauma of partition, including the mass displacement and violence that accompanied it, continues to resonate in Pakistani society. The subsequent decades witnessed attempts to create a homogenous Islamic identity, sometimes at the expense of religious diversity and minority rights. This process, although intended to forge national unity, resulted in the marginalisation of religious minorities and fueled tensions between different religious groups.

The rise of religious extremism presents another significant challenge for Pakistan's internal security and social harmony. Numerous extremist groups, with varying ideologies and levels of organisation, operate within the country, posing a threat to both the state and the population. These groups utilise religious rhetoric to justify violence and often exploit existing societal fault lines to advance their agendas. They target not only the government but also religious minorities, secular activists, and anyone perceived as opposing their ideology. The government's efforts to counter religious extremism have been met with mixed results. While security forces have engaged in numerous counterterrorism operations, the underlying causes of extremism, such as poverty, lack of education, and political grievances, often remain unaddressed. Furthermore, the government's responses to extremism have sometimes been heavy-handed, leading to accusations of human rights violations and further alienating specific segments of the population. The delicate balance between maintaining security and respecting human rights is a persistent challenge for the government.

Religious identity and politics are also evident in the electoral landscape. Religious parties, often advocating for stricter interpretations of Islamic law, hold varying levels of influence at the national and local levels. While some parties have contributed to political discourse, others have engaged in inflammatory rhetoric, contributing to social polarisation and undermining national unity. This political mobilisation along religious lines can further complicate efforts to promote inter-religious harmony and understanding. The government's attempts to manage the influence of religious parties and prevent their use of religion for political mobilisation are ongoing and often fraught with complex political considerations.

The government's policies towards religious minorities often reflect a complex interplay of political expediency, societal pressures, and international scrutiny. While some policies have aimed to protect minority rights, others have been criticised for perpetuating discrimination or failing to address the root causes of conflict. For example, the government's initiatives to promote interfaith dialogue have shown limited success in fostering genuine reconciliation and mutual understanding between different communities. The lack of trust between religious minorities and state institutions remains a significant obstacle to effective conflict resolution and reconciliation efforts. Creating inclusive governance structures that ensure the representation and participation of religious minorities in decision-making processes is crucial to achieving greater social harmony and reducing inter-religious tension. This includes promoting inclusive education systems that teach religious tolerance and respect for diversity from a young age and supporting religious organisations that actively promote interfaith dialogue and understanding.

The consequences of religious conflict extend far beyond the immediate victims. Such conflicts often lead to displacement, economic disruption, and lasting social trauma. They also damage Pakistan's international reputation and hinder its ability to attract foreign investment and engage in constructive international relations. The international community has repeatedly urged Pakistan to address its issues of religious freedom and minority rights. The failure to do so can result in sanctions or other forms of international pressure. The government faces a continuous challenge in balancing domestic policies with international human rights and religious freedom expectations.

In conclusion, understanding Pakistan's internal security challenges necessitates thoroughly analysing the complex interplay between religion, politics, and society. The country's religious diversity, coupled with the rise of extremism and persisting discrimination against minorities, poses significant challenges to social harmony and national security. Addressing these challenges requires a multi-pronged approach that combines effective security measures with policies that promote inclusivity, respect for religious freedom, and the rule of law. This includes strengthening the rule of law, improving law enforcement's impartiality in investigating and prosecuting crimes against minorities, promoting education and awareness about religious tolerance, and engaging in meaningful dialogue to build trust and reconciliation among different religious communities. Without tackling these fundamental issues, Pakistan's efforts to achieve lasting stability and enhance its global standing will remain significantly hampered. The path to a more secure and prosperous Pakistan requires a concerted effort to address the deep-seated societal divisions arising from religious identity, ensuring that all citizens, irrespective of their religious beliefs, can enjoy equal rights, opportunities, and security. Only then can Pakistan effectively navigate the complex geopolitical landscape and fully realise its potential.

Foreign Policy and Regional Relations Navigating Complex Alliances

Pakistan's foreign policy is a complex tapestry woven from threads of strategic necessity, historical baggage, and domestic political considerations. Its geographical location, bordering Afghanistan and Iran, and its proximity to India make it a crucial player in regional dynamics. It constantly navigates a precarious balance between competing interests and alliances. This delicate balancing act is further complicated by its internal security challenges, discussed in the preceding section, which significantly influence its foreign policy decisions and capabilities.

The relationship with India, characterised by a long history of conflict and mistrust, remains the central axis of Pakistan's foreign policy. The unresolved Kashmir dispute continues to cast a long shadow, periodically escalating into armed confrontations and hindering any significant progress towards lasting peace. Both nations possess nuclear weapons, adding an extremely dangerous layer to their rivalry. Despite intermittent attempts at dialogue and cooperation, deep-seated suspicions and historical grievances frequently undermine these efforts. The military build-up on both sides fuels an arms race, diverting scarce resources from critical development needs. The constant threat of conflict significantly impacts Pakistan's economic stability and its ability to focus on internal development. Furthermore, the ongoing disputes over water resources and other shared assets further strain bilateral relations and contribute to regional instability. While both countries recognise the need for peaceful resolution, the lack of trust and political will continues to hinder substantial progress.

The relationship with China has become a cornerstone of Pakistan's foreign policy. The China-Pakistan Economic Corridor (CPEC), a massive infrastructure project under the Belt and Road Initiative (BRI), symbolises this growing strategic partnership. CPEC has brought substantial investment into Pakistan, addressing infrastructural gaps and boosting economic growth, but concerns remain about its long-term financial sustainability and potential impact on Pakistan's sovereignty. The deep economic interdependence between the two countries has created a strong strategic alliance, which extends beyond economic ties to encompass military cooperation and diplomatic support. China's unwavering backing of Pakistan on the Kashmir issue provides crucial diplomatic leverage in international forums, significantly mitigating the isolation that Pakistan frequently faces from other major powers. However, this close alignment with China also carries potential risks, particularly as China's global influence expands and its geopolitical ambitions become increasingly assertive. This raises questions regarding Pakistan's ability to maintain an independent foreign policy, particularly if China's interests diverge from its own.

Pakistan's relations with the United States have been a rollercoaster ride, marked by periods of close cooperation and intense tension. Initially, a close ally during the Cold War, the relationship became strained after 9/11, despite Pakistan's cooperation in the war on terror. The U.S. support for India, especially in the defence sector, has increased Pakistan's security concerns and fueled a sense of mistrust. Furthermore, drone strikes within Pakistan's territory, undertaken by the U.S., have resulted in civilian casualties and heightened anti-American sentiment, further complicating the relationship. The U.S. strategy towards Afghanistan has also impacted the relationship, creating tensions stemming from differing approaches to regional stability and the handling of the Afghan Taliban. Despite these challenges, the U.S. remains a significant player in Pakistan's geopolitical landscape, providing access to certain technologies and engaging in efforts for regional stability. However, the fluctuating nature of this relationship leaves Pakistan frequently searching for a secure and balanced approach in its interactions with the US.

Pakistan's foreign policy extends beyond its immediate neighbours and key global players. Its membership in various international organisations, including the Organisation of Islamic Cooperation (OIC), the South Asian Association for Regional Cooperation (SAARC), and the

Shanghai Cooperation Organisation (SCO), reflects its aspiration to play a prominent role in global affairs. The OIC provides a platform for engagement with the Muslim world, allowing Pakistan to project its influence and advocate for issues pertinent to the Islamic community. SAARC, despite its limitations due to the India-Pakistan tension, allows for regional cooperation in certain areas. The SCO presents a new avenue for interaction with Central Asian states and China, enhancing its strategic partnerships and connectivity. However, participating in these organisations also presents challenges, including balancing national interests with collective goals and navigating complex regional dynamics. Pakistan's role in these multilateral platforms is essential to its foreign policy, highlighting its commitment to regional and international cooperation alongside its pursuit of national interests.

Furthermore, Pakistan's foreign policy is greatly influenced by its internal political landscape. The frequent changes in government, often accompanied by shifts in political priorities, can lead to inconsistencies and unpredictability in its foreign relations. The powerful military establishment also plays a significant role, shaping defence policies and influencing ties with key partners. This internal dynamic complicates Pakistan's external engagements, creating uncertainty for its allies and partners. The interplay between civilian and military leadership in foreign policy decision-making is an ongoing feature of Pakistan's political system.

Its strategic location and internal challenges further complicate Pakistan's role in regional conflicts. The country has been embroiled in various conflicts, either directly or indirectly, including Afghanistan and the wider regional instability. The Afghan conflict has had a particularly profound impact, impacting the country's internal security and foreign policy objectives. The influx of refugees, the spread of extremism across borders, and the fluctuating nature of the Afghan government have added complexity to Pakistan's security environment and its relationships with regional and global actors. The country attempts to balance its role as a neighbouring state with its need to protect its national interests. Its attempts at brokering peace and engaging in regional diplomacy are often complicated by the deeply entrenched conflicts and the competing interests of various regional and international actors. The cross-border dynamics have been further exacerbated by the presence of militant groups and the movement of fighters across borders. Pakistan's approach to this continuous challenge requires a careful strategy that recognises its internal security concerns and obligations towards regional stability.

Pakistan's efforts to balance its relations with competing powers are a constant challenge. For instance, the country's attempts to maintain good relations with the U.S. and China often necessitate navigating conflicting interests and geopolitical pressures. This balancing act requires careful diplomacy and a nuanced understanding of the global power dynamics. Pakistan must carefully strategise to avoid antagonising any of its key partners, especially as major global power balances shift. The country is acutely aware that overly close relationships with one power can damage its relationships with others, leading to potential isolation or compromising its national interests. Therefore, its foreign policy often seeks to maintain diverse relationships, enabling it to access broader opportunities and reducing its vulnerability to pressure from any single power. This multi-faceted approach calls for shrewd diplomatic negotiations and considerable political maneuvering to navigate a complex and potentially volatile geopolitical environment. The success of this balancing act will largely determine Pakistan's ability to secure its national interests and navigate a rapidly changing global landscape.

Military Capabilities and National Security Regional Dynamics

Pakistan's military is a significant force in South Asia, possessing a substantial conventional military alongside a nuclear arsenal. Understanding its capabilities is crucial to comprehending its role in regional security dynamics and its influence on foreign policy decisions. The country's military expenditure consistently ranks among the region's highest, reflecting its perceived security threats and the military's significant impact within the Pakistani state. This substantial investment has resulted in a reasonably well-equipped army, navy, and air force, capable of engaging in conventional and asymmetric warfare.

The Pakistan Army is the dominant military branch, historically playing a central role in national politics and foreign policy formulation. Its size and technological capabilities are considerable, although the quality of equipment and training varies across different units. The army's operational experience, gained through numerous internal security operations and border skirmishes, is extensive. However, criticisms persist regarding issues such as human rights abuses and allegations of extrajudicial killings during counter-terrorism operations. The army's capacity for large-scale conventional warfare remains a key aspect of Pakistan's regional power projection, though resource constraints and competing priorities necessitate careful resource allocation.

The Pakistan Navy, while smaller than the army, has undergone significant modernisation in recent years. Its acquisition of submarines and sophisticated naval vessels reflects an increasing emphasis on maritime security and power projection capabilities in the Indian Ocean region. This development is partly driven by the rising strategic importance of the region's sea lanes and Pakistan's interest in securing its coastline and offshore resources. However, challenges remain in maintaining and upgrading its fleet due to budgetary constraints and dependence on foreign suppliers.

The Pakistan Air Force (PAF) possesses a relatively modern fleet of fighter jets, albeit with a dependence on foreign suppliers for advanced weaponry and technology. The PAF's air superiority capabilities are essential in deterring potential aggression and cornerstone of Pakistan's overall military strategy. Technological upgrades and maintenance are ongoing concerns requiring substantial investment, like the Navy. The PAF's role in defending Pakistani airspace and supporting ground operations is crucial to national security.

Pakistan's nuclear arsenal is central to its military capabilities and a defining aspect of its regional role. Developed as a deterrent against India's nuclear capability, it represents a source of national pride and a considerable security concern for the international community. The exact size and sophistication of Pakistan's atomic stockpile are not publicly known, shrouded in secrecy for national security reasons. However, the arsenal fundamentally alters the regional security landscape, creating a strategic balance of power and potentially increasing the risk of escalation in any conflict with India.

The management and control of Pakistan's nuclear weapons program are subjects of ongoing debate and scrutiny. Concerns remain about the safety and security of the arsenal, its potential vulnerability to non-state actors, and the potential for proliferation. International efforts to promote non-proliferation and enhance safeguards have been met with a mixed response from Pakistan, with the country balancing its security needs with concerns regarding external intervention. This precarious balance represents a critical aspect of Pakistan's security and its interactions with the international community.

The relationship between Pakistan's military and civilian government is complex and historically fraught. The military has frequently intervened in civilian politics, establishing direct military rule several times. This influence permeates national security and foreign policy decision-making, leading to an intricate interplay between military and civilian interests. While democratic transitions have occurred, the military's powerful presence continues to shape the country's strategic direction. The extent of military influence over budget allocation, policy formulation, and operational decisions remains a subject of ongoing analysis and debate. Understanding this dynamic is crucial for comprehending Pakistan's policy choices and its behaviour in the international arena.

The annual military budget consumes substantial resources that could otherwise be used for social development and infrastructure projects. This diversion of funds has led to criticism regarding the opportunity costs of maintaining such a large military establishment. The trade-off between security needs and economic development is a persistent challenge for Pakistan. While the military argues that its strength is essential for national security, critics highlight the need for prioritisation and greater transparency in military spending. The allocation of resources reflects the country's security priorities, but also reflects the military's influence on national decision-making.

Pakistan's military capabilities significantly shape its regional relationships. The country's nuclear arsenal acts as a deterrent against India, impacting the dynamics of the South Asian security environment. Its conventional military capabilities influence its stance in regional conflicts, shaping its responses to internal security threats and its involvement in international coalitions. However, the size and focus of its military establishment also impact Pakistan's ability to focus on socio-economic development. Maintaining a large military and a nuclear program presents a significant opportunity cost and diverts resources that could be used to address poverty, education, healthcare, and infrastructure deficits. The country's commitment to military strength has long-term economic stability and sustainability implications.

Pakistan's military's influence extends beyond its immediate regional context, impacting global security. Its nuclear arsenal contributes to global non-proliferation concerns, while its involvement in counterterrorism efforts both domestically and internationally has both positive and negative consequences. Pakistan's engagement with international security organisations and cooperation with global powers in combating terrorism are essential to its role in international security. However, there are frequently tensions and concerns regarding its approach.

The interplay between Pakistan's internal security challenges, military capabilities, and regional dynamics creates a complex and often precarious security environment. The military's role in internal security operations, its influence on foreign policy, and its management of its nuclear arsenal all contribute to the overall security landscape. Understanding these interconnections is vital for comprehending Pakistan's actions and interactions with the international community. The country's approach to its security needs is intrinsically tied to its internal political environment, relationship with its neighbours, and position within the complex international system. Balancing these factors while addressing internal socio-economic issues remains a significant challenge for Pakistan. The future of Pakistan's security will undoubtedly depend on how successfully these interconnected aspects are managed and how the country navigates the inherent complexities of its strategic position.

Chapter 5
Indonesia, Malaysia, and Nigeria: Diverse Trajectories, Shared Challenges

Indonesia Consolidating Democracy and Managing Diversity

Since the fall of Suharto's authoritarian regime in 1998, Indonesia's journey has been a remarkable, albeit complex, case study in democratic consolidation. Transitioning from a centralised, highly controlled state to a multi-party democracy was challenging. The deeply ingrained culture of patronage, the legacy of corruption, and the sheer diversity of the Indonesian archipelago, comprising over 17,000 islands, hundreds of ethnic groups, and many religious beliefs, presented significant hurdles to building a stable and inclusive democracy.

A fragile political landscape characterised the initial years of democratic transition. The newly established institutions were often weak and vulnerable to manipulation, and the country struggled to establish a robust rule of law. The potential for ethnic and religious conflict loomed large, fueled by historical grievances and competing claims to power. The 1998 riots in Jakarta, triggered by the economic crisis and long-simmering ethnic tensions, served as a stark reminder of the fragility of the transition. The violence against the Chinese Indonesian community highlighted the vulnerability of minority groups and the potential for societal fracture along ethnic and religious lines.

However, despite these formidable obstacles, Indonesia has demonstrated a remarkable resilience. The country has successfully held several free and fair elections, demonstrating a commitment to democratic principles. Establishing the Constitutional Court, an independent judiciary, and a relatively free press have contributed to a more transparent and accountable government. While imperfections remain, and concerns about corruption and weak enforcement continue, the progress made in strengthening democratic institutions represents a significant achievement.

A crucial aspect of Indonesia's democratic consolidation has been its approach to managing its immense religious and ethnic diversity. Indonesia is the world's most populous Muslim-majority nation, but it also boasts significant Christian, Hindu, Buddhist, and other religious communities. The constitution guarantees freedom of religion, and the state officially adheres to a principle of secularism, though the relationship between religion and the state is complex and often contested. The government has implemented various policies to promote religious harmony and prevent interfaith conflict. These efforts include establishing interfaith dialogue forums, promoting religious education that emphasises tolerance and mutual understanding, and tackling religious extremism with law enforcement and community-based initiatives. The success of these policies is mixed, and sporadic outbreaks of religious violence persist, demonstrating the ongoing challenges involved in managing religious pluralism in a society with sincerely held religious beliefs.

The Indonesian government has actively attempted to foster a sense of national unity amidst this diversity. The concept of *Bhinneka Tunggal Ika* ("Unity in Diversity") is deeply embedded in the national consciousness, highlighting the need to embrace differences while maintaining national cohesion. However, this ideal faces constant pressure, particularly during political and economic instability. The manipulation of ethnic and religious differences for political gain remains a significant concern, and there is an ongoing need for concerted efforts to counter such divisive tactics.

Economic development has been another crucial factor in Indonesia's post-Suharto trajectory. The country has experienced significant economic growth in recent decades, although this growth has been uneven, with disparities between regions and social classes persisting. While poverty levels have fallen significantly, inequality remains a significant concern. The concentration of wealth in the hands of a relatively small elite, alongside the widespread corruption that pervades many aspects of Indonesian life, is a significant obstacle to inclusive economic growth. Government policies have sought to address these issues through initiatives to improve infrastructure, invest in human capital, and promote small and medium-sized enterprises (SMEs). However, the challenge of balancing economic growth with equitable distribution of wealth remains a critical long-term issue.

Several key policy initiatives implemented by successive Indonesian governments illustrate the complexities of managing diversity and promoting equitable development. The decentralisation program, launched in the early 2000s, aimed to devolve power from the central government to local governments. The rationale behind this initiative was to empower local communities, increase participation in governance, and tailor policies to meet regional specificities. However, the decentralisation program has had mixed results. While it has increased local autonomy, it has also led to inconsistencies in policy implementation and increased corruption in some regions. The lack of local capacity to manage the increased autonomy has led to challenges in many areas.

Indonesia's efforts to strengthen its human capital base through education and healthcare initiatives are crucial to its economic development strategy. Investments in education have increased, and programs aiming to improve the quality of primary and secondary education are ongoing. Improved healthcare infrastructure and increased access to medical services are also critical governmental goals. However, significant challenges persist, including disparities in access to quality education and healthcare based on geographic location and socioeconomic status. The country's rapidly growing population also significantly strains the education and healthcare systems.

The Indonesian government's commitment to fostering a more robust and inclusive economic environment is demonstrated in its efforts to support SMEs. SMEs constitute the backbone of the Indonesian economy, providing significant employment and contributing considerably to GDP growth. However, SMEs often face challenges related to access to finance, limited market access, and inadequate technology. The government has implemented numerous programs to address these constraints, providing financial support, business training, and assistance with market linkages. However, the effectiveness of these programs has been varied, and a considerable gap remains between the government's ambition and actual impact on the ground.

The challenge of promoting inclusive growth and reducing inequality remains one of Indonesia's most significant priorities. Despite substantial economic growth, the benefits have not always been shared equitably, leading to disparities in income, wealth, and access to opportunities. The concentration of wealth in urban areas and the persistent poverty in rural areas highlight these inequalities. The government has taken steps to address these issues through targeted poverty reduction programs, social safety nets, and investment in infrastructure in less-developed areas. However, achieving meaningful progress will require a sustained commitment to tackling corruption, strengthening governance, and ensuring that economic policies are designed to promote inclusivity.

In conclusion, Indonesia's journey since 1998 has been remarkable progress and persistent challenges. The country has made significant strides in consolidating its democracy, managing its incredible diversity, and promoting economic growth. However, the ongoing struggles with corruption, inequality, and the occasional flare-ups of ethnic and religious tensions demonstrate that the Indonesian democratic project is far from complete. The country's success in navigating these challenges will have important implications for its future, the broader region, and the global community. The ongoing interplay between political stability, economic development, and the management of diversity will continue to shape Indonesia's trajectory in the future. Understanding the complex dynamics within Indonesian society and the government's efforts to address them is essential for understanding the intricacies of this key player in Southeast Asian politics and the broader global landscape.

Malaysia Balancing Development and Political Stability

Malaysia's trajectory since independence in 1957 presents a compelling narrative of balancing economic development with political stability, albeit with significant complexities and ongoing challenges. Unlike Indonesia's tumultuous transition from authoritarianism, Malaysia's path has been characterised by a more gradual, albeit often controlled, evolution of its political system, intertwined with a remarkable economic transformation. The country's success in achieving high economic growth rates, particularly during the New Economic Policy (NEP) period, is frequently cited as a model for other developing nations. However, this achievement has been accompanied by persistent concerns regarding ethnic and economic inequalities, a complex relationship between the state and the dominant political party (the United Malays National Organisation, or UMNO), and ongoing debates regarding the balance between development and democratic principles.

The NEP, implemented in 1971 in the wake of racial riots, aimed to redress the economic imbalances between the Malay majority and the Chinese and Indian minorities. The policy involved affirmative measures to promote Malay participation in education, business, and government positions. While the NEP undeniably spurred significant economic advancement, it also fueled criticisms regarding its effectiveness and unintended consequences. Critics argue that the policy created a system of cronyism and reinforced existing inequalities by favouring Malay-owned businesses and limiting opportunities for non-Malays. This led to the emergence of a powerful Malay elite while perpetuating socioeconomic disparities across racial lines. The policy's long-term impact on Malaysian society continues to be debated, with some arguing that it fostered national unity, while others contend it entrenched racial divisions.

The UMNO-led coalition government has dominated the Malaysian political landscape for much of its post-independence history. While elections were held regularly, the dominance of UMNO, coupled with allegations of gerrymandering and electoral manipulation, cast doubts on the true extent of democratic competition. The ruling coalition maintained power through a skilful combination of patronage, clientelism, and co-optation of opposition forces. While ensuring political stability, this system stifled genuine political pluralism and limited the space for open dissent. The emergence of a vibrant civil society and opposition parties in recent decades has challenged UMNO's hegemony, leading to more competitive elections and increased political polarisation. However, the legacy of UMNO's long-term rule continues to shape the nation's political dynamics.

The economic success of Malaysia, particularly in the late 20th century, was primarily attributed to its export-oriented industrialisation strategy, focused on attracting foreign investment and developing export-driven industries. The government played a central role in guiding economic policy, providing incentives for foreign investors, and developing infrastructure. The country's strategic location, relatively skilled workforce, and political stability made it an attractive destination for foreign investment. While delivering substantial economic growth, this model resulted in a dualistic economy with significant disparities between rural and urban areas and between different ethnic groups. The concentration of wealth in the hands of a relatively small elite, particularly among those connected to the ruling party, fueled further criticism of the economic model's inclusivity.

Subsequent economic policies, aimed at achieving greater equity and inclusivity, involved diversification beyond export-oriented industries, focusing on developing small and medium-sized enterprises (SMEs) and promoting innovation-driven growth. The government implemented various initiatives, including training programs for SMEs, access to finance programs, and infrastructure improvements. The effectiveness of these initiatives has been mixed, and persistent challenges remain in addressing income inequality and regional disparities. The transition to a more knowledge-based economy requires substantial investment in human capital, particularly in education and technological skills, which is a key challenge for Malaysia to maintain its economic competitiveness.

Malaysia's commitment to education has been a significant part of its developmental strategy. The government has invested heavily in expanding access to education. However, questions remain about the quality of teaching and the effectiveness of educational reform policies in ensuring a skilled workforce capable of meeting the demands of a rapidly changing global economy. Issues of equity in access to quality education persist across ethnic and socioeconomic groups. The uneven distribution of resources and opportunities in the education system reflects broader systemic inequalities.

Healthcare is another crucial area influencing Malaysia's development trajectory. The country boasts a relatively well-developed healthcare system, with significant investments in public healthcare infrastructure and services. However, the ongoing challenges related to access to healthcare, particularly for rural populations and low-income groups, remain substantial. The rising cost of healthcare and the growing burden of chronic diseases also pose significant challenges to the sustainability of the healthcare system.

The rise of social media and the increasing interconnectedness of the global community have significantly impacted Malaysia's political landscape. Social media platforms have become crucial battlegrounds for political discourse, with government and opposition forces utilising them to mobilise support and disseminate their messages. The spread of misinformation and the potential for online hate speech have also become significant concerns, highlighting the need for effective media literacy initiatives and regulatory measures to address the challenges posed by the digital age. The government's efforts to balance freedom of expression with the need to maintain social stability in the digital sphere remain a significant balancing act.

Malaysia's foreign policy reflects its strategic location in Southeast Asia and its commitment to regional cooperation. The country plays an active role in ASEAN (the Association of Southeast Asian Nations), emphasising regional economic integration and security cooperation. Malaysia also maintains strong bilateral relationships with various countries across the globe, pursuing economic diplomacy and strategic partnerships to enhance its national interests. The balancing act between maintaining its national interests and navigating complex regional dynamics, including relations with neighbouring countries and major global powers, is a constant challenge.

In conclusion, Malaysia's experience provides a rich case study of the complexities of balancing economic development and political stability, particularly in a multi-ethnic and multicultural society. While the country has achieved remarkable economic success, significant challenges remain in addressing persistent inequalities, strengthening democratic institutions, and ensuring inclusive growth. The interplay between these factors will continue to shape Malaysia's future trajectory in the years to come, making its story a fascinating and critical study for understanding the multifaceted challenges of development in the 21st century. The country's ability to address these challenges effectively will determine its future and role in the broader Southeast Asian region and the global landscape. The success in balancing development and political stability in Malaysia will be crucial to its continued progress and prosperity. The ongoing efforts to address economic inequalities, strengthen democratic processes, and navigate the complex dynamics of a rapidly changing global environment will be crucial in shaping the future of this important Southeast Asian nation.

Nigeria Combating Terrorism and Promoting National Unity

Nigeria, Africa's most populous nation, presents a starkly different trajectory from Indonesia and Malaysia. While those nations have grappled with their own sets of challenges in balancing development with political stability, Nigeria's journey has been profoundly marked by a persistent struggle against violent extremism and deep-seated ethnic and religious divisions. This struggle significantly undermines its potential for sustainable economic growth and national unity. Understanding Nigeria's challenges requires examining the complex interplay between terrorism, ethnic conflict, economic disparities, and the government's responses to these interwoven crises.

The rise of Boko Haram in the northeast, a jihadist group aiming to establish an Islamic caliphate, has been a defining feature of Nigeria's recent history. Initially focusing on imposing strict religious observance, Boko

Haram's actions escalated into widespread violence, including bombings, kidnappings, and mass killings of civilians. The group's brutality has displaced millions, creating a humanitarian crisis of immense proportions. The insurgency has not only devastated the northeast region but has also destabilised neighbouring countries, highlighting the transnational nature of the threat. The group's tactics have evolved, employing increasingly sophisticated attack methods and utilising social media for propaganda and recruitment. The Nigerian military's response, while often criticised for human rights abuses and operational inefficiencies, has demonstrably achieved some successes in containing Boko Haram's territorial control and neutralising key commanders. However, the insurgency's persistence underscores the limitations of a purely military approach and the need for a comprehensive strategy that addresses the underlying root causes of the conflict.

Beyond Boko Haram, Nigeria faces other significant security threats, including farmer-herder clashes, banditry, and secessionist movements. Resource competition, land disputes, and long-standing ethnic grievances often fuel these conflicts. The competition for arable land and water resources, exacerbated by climate change, has intensified tensions between farming and pastoralist communities, leading to frequent violent clashes with devastating consequences. Similarly, banditry, characterised by armed robbery, kidnapping, and extortion, has become increasingly prevalent in many parts of the country, disrupting economic activity and instilling fear among the population. The rise of secessionist movements, particularly in the southeast, fueled by feelings of marginalisation and political exclusion, further complicates the security landscape.

The Nigerian government's approach to combating terrorism and promoting national unity has been multifaceted, encompassing military operations, security sector reforms, and various social and economic development initiatives. The military has been deployed to multiple conflict zones, engaging in counterinsurgency operations. However, challenges remain in terms of coordination, equipment, and training. Concerns have been consistently raised regarding human rights violations committed by security forces during counter-terrorism operations, further undermining trust between the government and affected communities. Security sector reform, aimed at improving security agencies' professionalism, accountability, and effectiveness, is crucial but faces significant obstacles. The lack of adequate funding, political will, and institutional capacity often hampers the implementation of reforms.

Alongside military efforts, the government has initiated numerous social and economic programs to address the root causes of conflict and promote national unity. These programs include education, healthcare, job creation, and poverty reduction initiatives. The government has invested in infrastructure projects to improve access to essential services, particularly in marginalised communities. Yet, the effectiveness of such initiatives has often been hampered by corruption, poor implementation, and lack of transparency. Furthermore, the scale of the challenges frequently outstrips the resources available, and the distribution of resources has sometimes exacerbated existing inequalities. The uneven distribution of development initiatives among different regions and ethnic groups often fuels further resentment and grievances, undermining the goal of national unity.

Economic inequality is a significant factor contributing to instability in Nigeria. The vast disparities between the wealthy elite and the impoverished majority are a source of social tension and political unrest. The concentration of wealth in the hands of a small segment of the population fuels resentment and frustration among those left behind, creating fertile ground for extremist ideologies and violent conflict. The country's dependence on oil revenues has also left its economy vulnerable to price fluctuations and hindered the development of other sectors. The lack of diversification of the economy has made it particularly susceptible to global economic shocks. Inefficient governance, corruption, and a weak regulatory framework further hinder economic growth and contribute to widespread poverty. The uneven distribution of resources and opportunities has exacerbated existing ethnic and regional divisions, fueling conflict and undermining social cohesion. Addressing these economic disparities is paramount to promoting sustainable peace and national unity.

The government's efforts to promote national unity are often hampered by the country's complex ethnic and religious landscape. Nigeria has hundreds of ethnic groups, each with a distinct cultural identity and political interests. While enriching the country's cultural tapestry, this diversity also poses considerable challenges to national integration. Political elites have often exploited deep-seated ethnic and religious tensions for their gain, further exacerbating divisions and hindering efforts to build national unity. The lack of inclusive governance and political representation has contributed to feelings of marginalisation and exclusion among certain groups, fueling resentment and conflict. Promoting national unity requires addressing the underlying grievances, promoting inter-ethnic dialogue, and fostering inclusive political participation. Establishing institutions that can effectively manage ethnic and religious diversity, ensure equitable representation, and promote intergroup understanding is crucial.

The role of traditional and religious leaders in mediating conflicts and promoting peacebuilding initiatives should not be underestimated. These leaders often command significant influence within their communities and can play a vital role in de-escalating tensions and promoting reconciliation. Their involvement in peacebuilding efforts can significantly resolve conflicts and foster a sense of shared identity and common purpose. However, it is also crucial to recognise the potential for manipulation and misuse of their authority, and measures should be implemented to ensure their impartiality and accountability.

In conclusion, Nigeria's challenges are deeply intertwined and demand a holistic approach. While military intervention has a role to play in combating terrorism, a comprehensive strategy must address the root causes of conflict, including economic inequality, ethnic tensions, and weak governance. Investing in education, healthcare, job creation, infrastructure, and fostering inclusive governance are crucial to promoting sustainable peace and national unity. Addressing the underlying grievances of different groups, promoting inter-group dialogue, and strengthening institutions that can manage diversity are vital components of building a more peaceful and unified Nigeria. The success of these efforts will shape Nigeria's future and have far-reaching implications for regional stability in West Africa. The journey toward achieving lasting peace and national unity in Nigeria remains a complex and demanding process that requires sustained commitment, innovative strategies, and a concerted effort from the government, civil society, and international partners. The path ahead is arduous, but the potential rewards of a peaceful and prosperous Nigeria are immense.

Comparative Analysis Common Themes and Divergent Paths

Despite their vastly different geographical locations and historical contexts, Indonesia, Malaysia, and Nigeria share some striking similarities in their post-colonial trajectories. All three are multi-ethnic, multi-religious societies that have wrestled with the complexities of nation-building in the shadow of inherited colonial structures. They have all embarked on ambitious development agendas, balancing economic growth with social equity and political stability. However, their approaches to these challenges and the resulting outcomes have diverged significantly. A comparative analysis reveals crucial lessons about the interplay between political systems, economic policies, societal cohesion, and external influences in shaping the destinies of these diverse nations.

One significant commonality is the role of religion in the public sphere. Indonesia, the world's most populous Muslim-majority nation, has constitutionally guaranteed religious freedom, yet the interplay between Islam and politics remains a delicate balance. While Islamic political parties have existed and gained influence at times, the predominantly secular nature of the Indonesian state has, so far, managed to prevent the emergence of a theocratic regime. Malaysia, similarly, navigates a delicate balance between its predominantly Muslim population and its constitutionally enshrined secularism. The government's policies, particularly those about religious affairs and education, often tread a fine line, aiming to accommodate diverse religious practices while maintaining a unified national identity. Nigeria, with its substantial Muslim and Christian populations, faces even greater religious complexities. The competition for resources, power, and political influence often falls along religious lines, fueling inter-communal tensions and contributing to the broader instability. While both Indonesia and Malaysia have, to a greater extent, found ways to incorporate religious diversity within a framework of national unity, Nigeria's struggle underscores the risks inherent in the lack of effective mechanisms for managing religious pluralism.

The influence of ethnicity adds another layer of complexity to the comparative analysis. Indonesia's vast archipelago, with its hundreds of ethnic groups, has historically grappled with regional autonomy and identity issues. The country's efforts to forge a unified national identity have sometimes come at the expense of local traditions and cultural practices. Malaysia also faces ethnic tensions, primarily between the Malay majority and the significant Chinese and Indian minorities. This tension has been a recurring theme in Malaysian politics, influencing policy decisions concerning affirmative action, economic opportunities, and language use. Nigeria's ethnic diversity is perhaps even more pronounced, with many ethnic groups often vying for political power and financial advantage. These ethnic divisions are central to the country's ongoing conflicts, creating significant obstacles to national unity and stable governance. The varying success in managing ethnic diversity highlights the importance of inclusive governance, equitable resource distribution, and robust mechanisms for conflict resolution.

Governance structures and institutional capacity also represent significant points of divergence. Indonesia's experience with authoritarian rule under Suharto, followed by a transition to democracy, demonstrates the challenges of institutional reform and the complexities of consolidating democratic norms. While maintaining a parliamentary system, Malaysia operates under a system with a dominant ruling coalition, which often raises concerns about political pluralism and opposition voices. Nigeria, despite its formal democratic framework, faces persistent challenges related to corruption, weak rule of law, and limited institutional capacity. The effectiveness of governance in all three countries affects the delivery of public services, economic development, and the overall well-being of their citizens. The capacity of these nations to tackle corruption, improve transparency and accountability, and strengthen their judicial systems directly impacts their prospects for sustained development and social harmony.

Economic development strategies also differ considerably. Indonesia has pursued a path of export-oriented industrialisation, supported by significant foreign investment. Malaysia has followed a similar trajectory, albeit with a more state-driven approach. However, both countries have faced challenges related to income inequality and the need for greater economic diversification. Nigeria, heavily reliant on its oil sector, has been vulnerable to fluctuating global oil prices and has struggled to develop its agricultural and industrial sectors. This dependence has created significant economic vulnerabilities and has contributed to the lack of diversification that makes these economies susceptible to external shocks. The divergent economic paths highlight the challenges of transitioning from a resource-based economy and the importance of sustainable and inclusive growth models.

The role of international relations and global influences cannot be overlooked. Indonesia and Malaysia have actively engaged in regional organisations, such as ASEAN, while maintaining strategic relationships with major global powers. As a significant player in the West African region, Nigeria has been involved in several regional initiatives, particularly those to tackle transnational security threats. The countries' participation in international organisations and foreign policy choices has influenced their domestic politics, economic opportunities, and overall standing in the global community. Their engagement with international actors and organisations demonstrates opportunities and challenges regarding resource acquisition and the complexities of navigating the global political landscape.

In conclusion, a comparative analysis of Indonesia, Malaysia, and Nigeria reveals everyday challenges and divergent paths. While all three countries have navigated the complexities of nation-building in multi-ethnic, multi-religious societies, their approaches to governance, economic development, and the management of religious and ethnic diversity have yielded vastly different outcomes. The role of religion, ethnicity, and governance in shaping their trajectories underscores the crucial importance of inclusive political systems, equitable economic policies, and strong institutions in achieving sustainable development and fostering social cohesion. The lessons learned from these diverse experiences offer valuable insights into the challenges and opportunities confronting many other developing nations across the globe. The comparative study of these nations provides a complex, nuanced understanding of the multiple factors impacting the success or failure of nation-building in a globalised world. Further research into the specifics of each nation's policies, social dynamics, and international relations will enrich our understanding of these multifaceted trajectories. These nations' ongoing evolution promises to continue providing valuable case studies for scholars and policymakers alike.

Regional and International Roles Engaging with the Global Community

Despite their internal differences, Indonesia, Malaysia, and Nigeria actively participate in the global community, shaping and being shaped by international relations. Their engagement varies depending on their geopolitical positions, national interests, and historical experiences. As the world's largest archipelagic nation and the most populous Muslim-majority country, Indonesia wields considerable influence within Southeast Asia and beyond. Its engagement in regional organisations like ASEAN (Association of Southeast Asian Nations) is pivotal to the bloc's stability and economic growth. Indonesia has consistently championed ASEAN's centrality in regional affairs, advocating for a rules-based order and promoting peaceful conflict resolution. This commitment is evident in Indonesia's proactive role in mediating regional disputes, exemplified by its efforts to facilitate dialogue between conflicting parties in Myanmar and other regional flashpoints. Moreover, Indonesia's participation in the East

Asia Summit (EAS), which includes major global powers like the United States and China, allows it to navigate the complex power dynamics of the Indo-Pacific region, furthering its influence on regional and international issues.

Beyond ASEAN, Indonesia's global presence extends through its active participation in the United Nations, the G20, and other multilateral forums. Indonesia's tenure as the G20 president in 2022 underscored its commitment to global governance and its willingness to take on leadership roles on crucial international issues such as climate change, sustainable development, and pandemic preparedness. Its foreign policy emphasises the promotion of peaceful coexistence, multilateralism, and resolving global challenges through cooperation. This commitment translates into significant contributions to UN peacekeeping operations and active participation in human rights, counter-terrorism, and humanitarian aid initiatives. The Indonesian government's sustained focus on strengthening its diplomatic ties with key countries across the globe, including the US, China, and several European nations, demonstrates its strategic approach to navigating the intricate web of international relations and further solidifies its position as a key player on the world stage.

Despite its smaller size than Indonesia, Malaysia plays a significant regional role, particularly within ASEAN. Its economic success, underpinned by a history of pragmatic and export-oriented policies, has given it considerable weight in the regional economic landscape. Malaysia's active involvement in initiatives such as the Regional

Comprehensive Economic Partnership (RCEP) reflects its dedication to boosting regional trade and financial integration. Furthermore, Malaysia's commitment to strengthening intra-ASEAN cooperation, especially in infrastructure development and digital connectivity, has earned it significant respect. Beyond ASEAN, Malaysia maintains close relationships with several key global players, engaging actively in multilateral dialogues and initiatives. While generally maintaining a non-aligned stance in international geopolitics, Malaysia has sought to utilise its diplomatic leverage to promote its national interests and contribute to global stability. However, Malaysia's involvement in global affairs has sometimes been inconsistent, reflecting the often shifting political landscape at home and internal debates surrounding its international positioning.

As Africa's most populous nation, Nigeria dominates regional and continental affairs. Its influence is rooted in its economic significance, large population, and geopolitical location in West Africa. Nigeria's engagement in the Economic Community of West African States (ECOWAS) is critical to the organisation's success, playing a central role in maintaining regional stability and advancing economic integration. Nigeria's military capabilities and willingness to intervene in regional conflicts have earned it a reputation as a significant security provider. However, Nigeria's internal challenges, including insecurity, corruption, and ethnic tensions, have sometimes hampered its ability to reach its full potential on the regional and continental stages. Nevertheless, Nigeria's commitment to strengthening regional cooperation, particularly in counter-terrorism efforts and tackling cross-border challenges like trafficking, remains significant.

Nigeria's international presence extends beyond Africa. It actively participates in the UN, the African Union, and the Commonwealth, advocating for African interests on the global stage. Its relationship with global powers is often complex, influenced by historical factors and its strategic importance in the worldwide energy markets. Its diplomatic efforts usually focus on securing development assistance and investment and projecting a positive image of Nigeria abroad. Nigeria's foreign policy frequently seeks to balance its engagement with Western countries and its relations with emerging powers, attempting to leverage diverse partnerships to promote its national interests. However, the country's economic volatility and ongoing internal conflicts pose significant challenges to its ability to fully realise its potential as a leading player in the global arena.

Indonesia, Malaysia, and Nigeria's varying regional and international engagement degrees illustrate the complex interplay between internal dynamics and external relations. While all three nations strive to shape regional and global agendas, their influence is influenced by their internal stability, economic strength, and the effectiveness of their diplomatic strategies. Their participation in regional organisations reflects their commitment to multilateralism and recognition of regional cooperation's importance in addressing shared challenges such as economic development, security threats, and environmental protection. However, their foreign policy approaches differ based on historical experiences, geopolitical interests, and national priorities. The complex global landscape necessitates a nuanced understanding of these nations' roles, recognising their opportunities and limitations. A continued examination of their foreign policy choices and their involvement in regional and global initiatives is essential to understanding the ever-evolving dynamics of international relations within the broader context of the Muslim world and the developing nations. This ongoing evolution requires continuous observation and analysis to fully grasp these nations' impact on the global stage and the challenges they face in achieving their international ambitions. The complexities of these nations' internal and external challenges are interwoven and should be studied collectively for a comprehensive understanding of their evolving roles in the international community.

Chapter 6
Iran and Bangladesh: Unique Challenges and Emerging Roles

Iran Navigating International Sanctions and Regional Tensions

Iran's intricate geopolitical landscape is defined by a complex interplay of internal political dynamics, a controversial nuclear program, and deeply entrenched regional rivalries. Understanding Iran's current position requires a nuanced examination of its historical trajectory, ideological underpinnings, and the consequences of its foreign policy choices. The Islamic Revolution of 1979 fundamentally reshaped Iran's domestic and foreign policies, establishing a theocratic system governed by the Supreme Leader and a complex power-sharing arrangement between various institutions. While exhibiting a degree of internal stability, this system has also been characterised by periods of internal political struggle and factionalism, often impacting its external relations. The clerical establishment's emphasis on Islamic ideals and anti-Western sentiment has significantly shaped its approach to international relations, leading to periods of heightened tension with the West and increased engagement with regional actors often perceived as adversaries by Western powers.

The Iranian nuclear program has been a central point of contention in Iran's relationship with the international community. While Iran maintains that its nuclear ambitions are purely for peaceful purposes, namely energy generation and medical research, the international community, particularly the United States and its allies, has expressed deep concern over the potential for Iran to develop nuclear weapons. This concern stems from Iran's past concealment of its nuclear activities, its refusal to comply with international safeguards fully, and its rhetoric related to the annihilation of Israel. The resulting international sanctions, imposed by the United Nations Security Council, the European Union, and the United States, have significantly impacted Iran's economy, severely restricting its access to global financial markets and hindering its ability to engage in international trade. These sanctions have exacerbated Iran's internal economic challenges, fueling inflation, unemployment, and widespread public dissatisfaction.

These sanctions have been profound, impacting various sectors of the Iranian economy. The oil and gas industry, a crucial source of revenue for the Iranian government, has been severely affected, leading to a reduction in oil exports and a significant decline in government revenues. This has, in turn, limited the government's capacity to fund essential social programs and infrastructure projects, further contributing to public discontent. The sanctions have also hindered Iran's access to advanced technologies, hindering its progress in various sectors, including its nuclear program, as acquiring essential components and expertise has become significantly more challenging. This economic hardship has contributed substantially to Iran's social unrest and political instability.

Iran's regional involvement further complicates its international relations. Iran supports various regional actors that are often considered adversaries by the West, notably Hezbollah in Lebanon, Hamas in Gaza, and various Shiite militias in Iraq and Syria. This support, provided through financial assistance, military training, and the provision of advanced weaponry, has been a significant factor contributing to regional instability and fueling ongoing conflicts. Iran's regional policies are primarily motivated by strategic interests aimed at countering the influence of its regional rivals, Saudi Arabia, and projecting its power across the region. This projection of power, however, often conflicts with the interests of other regional and international actors, creating a highly volatile and unpredictable situation. Iran's actions in the region are frequently condemned by the West, which views its involvement as destabilising and counterproductive to peace and security initiatives.

The interplay between Iran's nuclear ambitions, its regional involvement, and the resulting international sanctions has created a complex and dynamic security environment. The 2015 Joint Comprehensive Plan of Action (JCPOA), the Iran nuclear deal, offered a brief respite from escalating tensions. This multinational agreement limited Iran's nuclear program in exchange for the lifting of international sanctions. However, the JCPOA's lifespan was relatively short, with the United States withdrawing from the agreement under the Trump administration in 2018 and re-imposing sanctions. This withdrawal significantly hampered international efforts to manage Iran's nuclear program and exacerbated existing tensions. Subsequent attempts to revive the deal have been unsuccessful, leaving the future of the agreement uncertain and the potential for further escalation ever-present.

Despite the challenges posed by international sanctions and regional tensions, Iran has tried to diversify its global relationships. It has strengthened its ties with Russia and China, engaging in extensive economic and security cooperation with both countries. These partnerships provide Iran with alternative avenues for accessing resources, technologies, and political support, mitigating its dependence on international markets to some extent and reducing its vulnerability to Western pressure. The growing partnership between Iran, Russia, and China presents a significant geopolitical challenge to the existing world order.

However, these partnerships are not without their complexities. While these alliances have provided Iran with strategic benefits, there are potential risks. Iran's close relationship with Russia, for example, has exposed it to some of the international consequences stemming from Russia's invasion of Ukraine. Furthermore, the economic benefits of these partnerships may not fully compensate for the financial losses incurred due to the ongoing sanctions. The strategic alignment of interests between Iran, Russia, and China is also not without its inherent contradictions and potential for future tensions.

The future of Iran's relationship with the international community remains uncertain. A resolution to the nuclear standoff remains elusive, and the country's regional involvement continues to fuel instability. While Iran's engagement with Russia and China provides some level of geopolitical balance, it also entails substantial risks and potential long-term implications. The international community faces a difficult task in managing its relationship with Iran, balancing the need to contain Iran's nuclear ambitions and address its regional behaviour with the desire to de-escalate tensions and potentially open channels for constructive dialogue. The economic consequences of sanctions for the Iranian populace and the political implications of Iran's regional actions are factors that cannot be ignored in any attempt at conflict resolution.

Furthermore, Iran's internal political dynamics remain a critical factor in shaping its foreign policy. The ongoing power struggle between hardliners and reformers within the Iranian political system, alongside the societal pressures created by economic hardship, could significantly impact Iran's future foreign policy trajectory. Understanding the internal political landscape and the different factions within the Iranian political system is crucial for forecasting Iran's future actions and responses to international pressure. The potential for internal political instability could create a more confrontational or conciliatory approach towards the West and other regional actors.

The path forward requires a multi-pronged approach. International pressure on Iran's nuclear program must be coupled with diplomatic efforts aimed at de-escalating regional tensions and finding common ground on critical regional issues. A renewed focus on diplomacy, including a potential revival of the JCPOA or the negotiation of a new framework, is essential to prevent further escalation and encourage dialogue. Simultaneously, addressing the economic and humanitarian consequences of sanctions is vital to reducing societal unrest and fostering a more conducive environment for constructive engagement. The international community must be prepared for a prolonged and complex engagement with Iran, requiring patience, resilience, and a willingness to explore many diplomatic avenues. A sustainable and stable resolution can be achieved only through a comprehensive strategy considering the interplay of internal political dynamics, regional conflicts, and international sanctions. This complex situation demands continued analysis and a deep understanding of the actors and factors to determine the best path towards a more peaceful and stable future for Iran and the broader Middle East.

Economic Development and International Engagement Balancing Self Reliance and Cooperation

In contrast to Iran's tumultuous geopolitical journey, Bangladesh presents a narrative of remarkable economic progress interwoven with significant developmental challenges. Its post-independence history is marked by periods of political instability, punctuated by military coups and periods of democratic rule. While hindering sustained economic growth at times, this political volatility has not entirely stifled Bangladesh's remarkable transformation from a predominantly agrarian economy to one increasingly reliant on manufacturing and export-oriented industries. For instance, the country's garment industry has become a global powerhouse, contributing significantly to its GDP and providing employment for millions. However, this success story is not without its complexities and shadows. While a significant engine of economic growth, the garment sector has also been criticised for its labour practices and safety standards, raising concerns about worker exploitation and human rights.

Bangladesh's economic development strategy has focused on export-led growth and relies heavily on the ready-made garment (RMG) sector. This sector's success is a testament to Bangladesh's strategic focus on attracting foreign investment and integrating into the global value chains. The country has leveraged its low labour costs and relatively liberal trade policies to attract substantial foreign direct investment (FDI), particularly from East Asian countries. This approach, however, has also created vulnerabilities. Overdependence on a single sector exposes the economy to global economic shocks and fluctuations in demand for ready-made garments. The COVID-19 pandemic, for example, severely impacted the RMG industry, leading to job losses and a significant slowdown in economic growth. This underscored the need for diversification and a less reliance on a single industry. Consequently, Bangladesh has begun to prioritise other sectors, including information technology, pharmaceuticals, and agricultural processing. The development of these sectors, however, requires substantial investments in infrastructure, technology, and human capital development.

Pursuing economic self-reliance has been a central theme in Bangladesh's economic development strategy. However, achieving this goal requires a delicate balancing act. While the government has promoted domestic industries and sought to reduce reliance on imports, the country also recognises the importance of international cooperation and participation in global trade. This involves a strategic engagement with international organisations like the World Bank, the International

Monetary Fund (IMF), and various development partners. These organisations have provided crucial financial and technical assistance, supporting infrastructure development, education reforms, and poverty reduction programs. The relationship, however, is not without its challenges. Negotiations with international financial institutions often involve structural adjustment programs that may have unintended social and economic consequences for specific population segments.

Despite its impressive growth trajectory, Bangladesh still faces significant socio-economic challenges. Poverty, inequality, and environmental degradation remain persistent issues. A large portion of the population still lives below the poverty line, and access to quality education, healthcare, and basic infrastructure remains unevenly distributed. Rapid urbanisation has created overcrowded cities, straining resources and increasing pollution and environmental challenges. Addressing these challenges requires a multi-faceted approach involving investments in education, healthcare, infrastructure, and social safety nets.

Furthermore, climate change poses a significant threat to Bangladesh's economic development. As one of the most vulnerable countries to climate change impacts, Bangladesh faces frequent natural disasters, including cyclones, floods, and droughts. These events cause significant economic losses and displacement, hindering progress toward poverty reduction and sustainable development. Adapting to climate change, investing in climate-resilient infrastructure, and mitigating greenhouse gas emissions are paramount for long-term economic stability.

Bangladesh's engagement with international organisations has been instrumental in its development journey. The country's participation in international trade forums and adherence to global norms and standards have been crucial in promoting its integration into the global economy. Its involvement in the World Trade Organisation (WTO) has facilitated access to international markets. At the same time, collaborations with regional organisations like the South Asian Association for Regional Cooperation (SAARC) have promoted regional trade and cooperation. However, navigating the complex geopolitical landscape requires careful balancing of national interests and international commitments.

The interplay between economic development and international engagement is particularly complex in Bangladesh's political landscape. The country's political stability, characterised by periods of both democratic rule and authoritarian tendencies, has sometimes impacted its international relations and ability to attract foreign investment and development assistance. Maintaining political stability and strengthening democratic institutions are, therefore, crucial for ensuring sustainable economic growth and successful international engagement.

Comparing Iran and Bangladesh highlights the diversity of challenges and opportunities Muslim-majority countries face in the 21st century. Iran, with its rich history and abundant natural resources, has struggled with the consequences of political isolation, international sanctions, and regional conflicts. These external factors have hindered its pursuit of economic self-reliance, while its attempts to engage with the global community have been fraught with difficulties. On the other hand, Bangladesh has pursued a more outward-oriented approach, leveraging its strategic location and low labour costs to achieve remarkable economic growth. However, it still faces significant developmental challenges, including poverty, inequality, and environmental degradation.

Both countries, however, share a common challenge: the need to balance the pursuit of economic self-reliance with the imperative of international cooperation. Navigating the complexities of the globalised world requires a strategic approach that involves engagement with international organisations, participation in global trade, and a commitment to sustainable development goals. The successful management of this balance will be crucial in shaping the future trajectory of Iran and Bangladesh, and indeed, many other developing nations are navigating the complexities of the 21st-century global order. Their experiences offer valuable lessons for other developing countries grappling with similar economic development issues, political stability, and international engagement. The path towards prosperity requires effective monetary policies, robust political institutions, sustainable social policies, and a nuanced understanding of the global economic and geopolitical landscape. A deep understanding of both internal and external factors – including political stability, social cohesion, resource management, and international relations – is vital for crafting effective long-term development strategies.

The future of both Iran and Bangladesh depends on their ability to manage internal challenges while effectively engaging with the global community. This requires a sophisticated understanding of the international economic system, the political landscape, and the intricacies of international cooperation. Developing a robust framework for sustainable growth that incorporates environmental concerns, social equity, and political stability remains paramount. The role of technology, innovation, and human capital development cannot be overstated in shaping the trajectory of these nations in the coming decades. Furthermore, the ability to adapt to rapid globalisation, navigate geopolitical shifts, and leverage international partnerships will influence their economic prospects and overall geopolitical standing. Their evolving roles on the global stage will continue to be shaped by their ability to address internal challenges, embrace opportunities for international cooperation, and create sustainable pathways to economic and social progress. The ongoing interplay between domestic reforms, international engagement, and the global financial and political climate will continue to define these two nations' unique challenges and emerging roles in the future. Continued research and analysis of these complex dynamics are crucial for comprehending the evolving narratives of Iran and Bangladesh within the broader context of global politics and economics.

Religious Identity and Political Ideology A Unique Combination

The intertwining of religious identity and political ideology forms the bedrock of Iranian society and governance, a complex tapestry woven from centuries of historical and cultural influences. Unlike many nations where religion and state are formally separated, Iran's system is fundamentally theocratic, with the Supreme Leader, a religious figure, holding ultimate authority. This unique structure profoundly impacts the nation's political landscape, domestic policies, and interactions with the global community. The role of the clergy, specifically the Shi'a clergy, in political decision-making is pervasive, extending from the highest echelons of power down to local governance. This influence is not merely symbolic; it permeates every aspect of public life, from legislation and law enforcement to education and social norms.

The Constitution of the Islamic Republic of Iran, adopted in 1979 following the revolution, formally establishes the principle of velayat-e faqih, or the jurist's guardianship. This doctrine asserts the authority of a qualified religious scholar (faqih) to rule and interpret Islamic law. The Supreme Leader, selected from among the most senior religious figures, embodies this authority and holds ultimate power, overseeing the military, appointing key judges, and significantly influencing economic policy. This structure differs considerably from secular democratic models, where power is distributed among elected officials and a separation of church and state exists.

The influence of religious figures extends beyond the highest echelons of government. The Assembly of Experts, responsible for electing and removing the Supreme Leader, comprises senior clerics. The Guardian Council, which vets all legislation to ensure compliance with Islamic law, also has a significant clerical presence. This ensures that religious principles are consistently integrated into the legislative process, influencing everything from personal freedoms to economic regulations. The impact on social life is equally profound. Spiritual laws govern marriage, divorce, inheritance, and personal conduct. These laws often differ significantly from secular societies, creating a unique social framework.

The government's policies towards religious minorities, particularly those outside the Shi'a faith, are complex and often contentious. While the Constitution guarantees religious freedom to certain minority groups, the extent of this freedom is usually limited. Sunni Muslims, for example, while recognised as a significant minority, have faced restrictions on their religious practices and political participation. Other religious groups, such as Christians, Jews, and Zoroastrians, are also granted limited recognition, but they also face challenges. The level of tolerance and the specific restrictions imposed can vary over time, often influenced by political considerations and broader social trends.

The interplay between religious identity and political ideology is not always harmonious. Despite the official ideology promoting a unified and cohesive Islamic identity, tensions and divisions exist. These divisions often manifest themselves along different theological interpretations, or between those who prioritise religious adherence strictly and those advocating for a more moderate approach to Islamic principles within modern life. While often not openly expressed due to political constraints, internal disagreements influence political dynamics and policy-making processes. Understanding these internal tensions is crucial to analysing the country's political landscape.

The Iranian government employs various measures to reinforce its theocratic ideology and influence over society. These measures include rigorous media censorship, control over education systems to promote a specific religious worldview, and using religious institutions to mobilise social support for government policies. The government also sponsors religious events, promotes religious education, and uses religious discourse to legitimise its authority and policies. The effectiveness and reach of these measures vary across different social strata and geographic areas.

Conversely, resistance to the government's theocratic rule also exists. At the same time, direct opposition is often met with repression, and subtle forms of resistance persist, usually manifested in cultural practices or interpretations of religious texts. These forms of resistance underscore the complexity of the relationship between religious identity and political ideology. It is not a monolithic relationship but a fluid and constantly evolving dynamic.

Examining specific religious practices provides further insight into Iran's unique religious identity and political ideology. The observation of religious rituals, such as Friday prayers, often serves as a platform for political messaging and mobilisation. Religious holidays are also used to reinforce the government's narrative. However, it's equally vital to note that the state's influence isn't absolute; religious practices often exist between official sanction and individual interpretation, creating a complex picture of religious observance and its intersection with political life.

This unique combination has profoundly affected Iranian society. It has shaped social norms, economic policies, and international relations. The government's emphasis on self-reliance, driven partly by religious principles of independence and rejection of Western influence, has influenced its economic development strategy. Similarly, its foreign policy, often perceived as aggressive or confrontational by some, can also be interpreted through the lens of religious ideology and national identity.

In conclusion, Iran's religious identity and political ideology interplay is complex and dynamic. It is not simply a matter of religion influencing politics; it is a deeply interwoven relationship where religion forms the foundation of the political system itself. Understanding this relationship is critical to comprehending Iran's domestic policies, foreign relations, and role in the broader global context. While the theocratic system maintains its authority through various measures, the subtle and overt forms of resistance and differing interpretations within the religious community reveal the fluid nature of this unique synthesis of religious belief and political power. The tension between religious orthodoxy and individual interpretation continues to shape the Iranian political landscape, influencing its future trajectory significantly. This complex interplay will likely continue to define Iran's domestic and international relations for the foreseeable future. Further research needs to consider the evolving socio-political dynamics within the country, paying close attention to the changing demographics and the ever-evolving attitudes toward religion and the state. Only by acknowledging the complexities of this relationship can we fully understand Iran's current and future direction.

Bangladesh Managing Rapid Growth and Addressing Social Issues

Bangladesh's remarkable economic progress over the past few decades presents a compelling case study in rapid development and its attendant social complexities. From a nation grappling with widespread poverty and dependence on foreign aid, Bangladesh has transformed into a burgeoning economy, a significant player in the global garment industry, and a nation striving to improve the lives of its citizens. However, this rapid growth has not been without its challenges. The country continues to grapple with significant social issues, including high population density, persistent poverty and inequality, and the need for substantial improvements in education and healthcare.

The roots of Bangladesh's economic transformation lie in several key factors. The Ready-Made Garment (RMG) industry, employing millions of workers, predominantly women, has been a significant driver of export earnings and economic growth. This sector's success is inextricably linked to global supply chains, highlighting the country's integration into the international economy. However, this dependence also makes the Bangladeshi economy vulnerable to global economic fluctuations and shifts in consumer demand. The government has actively promoted the RMG sector through various policy measures, including export incentives, infrastructure development, and efforts to attract foreign investment.

Nevertheless, the sector's reliance on low-wage labour raises ethical concerns regarding worker rights and working conditions. The Rana Plaza tragedy in 2013, a catastrophic building collapse in which hundreds of garment workers perished, served as a stark reminder of the urgent need for improved worker safety regulations and enforcement. Subsequent reforms and increased international scrutiny have led to some improvements, but challenges remain in ensuring fair labour practices throughout the industry.

Beyond the RMG sector, Bangladesh has also witnessed growth in other economic areas, such as agriculture, remittances from overseas Bangladeshi workers, and the burgeoning information technology sector. Infrastructure investments, including transportation and communication network improvements, have facilitated economic activity and regional integration. The government's emphasis on microfinance initiatives has empowered women entrepreneurs and fostered entrepreneurship at the grassroots level. However, access to credit and financial services remains limited for many, particularly in rural areas. Furthermore, uneven distribution of wealth continues to be a significant obstacle to inclusive growth. A substantial portion of the population remains impoverished, and inequality gaps persist between urban and rural areas and among different socioeconomic groups.

Addressing the issue of poverty and inequality requires a multi-pronged approach. The government has implemented various poverty reduction programs, including social safety nets, subsidised food programs, and initiatives to improve access to education and healthcare. However, the effectiveness of these programs varies, and challenges remain in terms of reach, efficiency, and sustainability. Corruption, a pervasive problem throughout many Bangladeshi sectors, undermines the impact of government programs. The government's anti-corruption efforts have yielded mixed results, and widespread corruption remains a significant barrier to progress. Addressing this challenge requires a concerted effort across government institutions, law enforcement agencies, and civil society.

Population growth is another significant challenge for Bangladesh—the country's high population density pressures resources, infrastructure, and social services. Government initiatives focused on family planning and women's empowerment have shown some success in lowering fertility rates, yet the population continues to grow. The government has promoted various family planning methods, improved access to healthcare services, and undertaken public awareness campaigns to encourage smaller family sizes. However, cultural norms and societal beliefs continue to influence family size decisions, making it challenging to reduce population growth rapidly. Furthermore, the high population density exacerbates existing challenges related to urbanisation, environmental degradation, and resource competition.

Education is a crucial investment for Bangladesh's future. While progress has been made in increasing school enrollment rates, particularly among girls, significant disparities remain between different regions and socioeconomic groups. The quality of education, particularly in rural areas, remains a pressing concern. Government efforts are ongoing to improve educational infrastructure, teacher training, and curriculum development. However, challenges remain in providing equitable access to quality education for all, particularly in remote and underserved communities. Addressing these challenges requires substantial investment in teacher training, improvements to school infrastructure, and efforts to create a more equitable education system that caters to the needs of diverse learners.

Healthcare remains another area requiring significant investment. Access to healthcare services, particularly quality healthcare, varies significantly across regions. Rural areas often lack adequate healthcare facilities and trained medical professionals, leading to poorer health outcomes among rural populations. The government has launched numerous healthcare initiatives, including vaccination programs, improved access to primary healthcare services, and efforts to combat infectious diseases. However, significant challenges remain in improving the quality and accessibility of healthcare for all citizens. Strengthening the primary healthcare system, improving sanitation, and investing in training and retaining healthcare professionals are crucial steps in addressing these challenges.

Climate change poses a significant threat to Bangladesh's sustainable development. The country is highly vulnerable to the impacts of climate change, including sea-level rise, extreme weather events, and increased flooding. The government has implemented various adaptation and mitigation strategies, including investment in flood control measures, early warning systems, and climate-resilient infrastructure. However, the scale of the challenge necessitates greater international cooperation and investment in climate-resilient development strategies. The country also faces difficulties managing its substantial rivers and efficiently managing water resources for agriculture and consumption. Effective water resource management is crucial for sustainable development, particularly in the face of climate change and increasing water scarcity.

In conclusion, Bangladesh's economic progress is undeniable, but it still faces significant challenges in managing its rapid growth and addressing social issues. Balancing rapid economic development with social equity, sustainable resource management, and effective governance is a complex endeavour that demands a strategic, multi-faceted approach. Continuous investments in education, healthcare, and infrastructure, coupled with effective governance, robust anti-corruption measures, and strategic climate adaptation policies, are essential for achieving inclusive and sustainable development in Bangladesh. The success of these endeavours will largely determine the nation's ability to translate its economic progress into sustained improvements in the quality of life for all its citizens. The continuing challenge is not just economic growth, but ensuring that the benefits of that growth are shared equitably and sustainably, paving the way for a more prosperous and equitable future.

Foreign Policy and Regional Influence Expanding International Ties

Bangladesh's foreign policy, traditionally characterised by a non-aligned stance, has undergone a significant evolution in recent years, reflecting its growing economic clout and strategic ambitions. The nation's pursuit of economic development has been intricately linked to its engagement with the international community, particularly through increased trade and foreign investment. This outward orientation has broadened Bangladesh's diplomatic ties, resulting in a more multifaceted and assertive foreign policy.

One of the most significant aspects of Bangladesh's foreign policy is its commitment to multilateralism. As a member of numerous international organisations, including the United Nations, the South Asian Association for Regional Cooperation (SAARC), and the Organisation of Islamic Cooperation (OIC), Bangladesh actively participates in global governance and international forums. Its participation in these organisations provides a platform for promoting its national interests, advocating for its priorities on the global stage, and fostering cooperation with other countries. For example, Bangladesh's involvement in UN peacekeeping missions underscores its commitment to international peace and security and enhances its international standing. The country's contribution to peacekeeping operations demonstrates its willingness to actively maintain global stability, improve its soft power, and build relationships with various countries.

However, Bangladesh's participation in multilateral fora is not without its limitations. Navigating competing interests within these organisations, particularly in regional forums like SAARC, which political tensions have plagued, requires significant diplomatic dexterity. Bangladesh's efforts to balance its engagement with major powers like the United States and China present further complexities. Balancing these relationships requires skilful diplomacy to ensure that Bangladesh's national interests are not compromised and that it does not become entangled in great power rivalries.

Bilateral relations are a cornerstone of Bangladesh's foreign policy. Due to their shared border and extensive historical connections, close ties with India have been paramount. However, this relationship has tensions, often centred around border disputes, water-sharing agreements, and migration issues. Managing these contentious issues while preserving mutually beneficial trade, development, and security cooperation is a key priority for Bangladesh's foreign policy. The complex interplay between cooperation and competition defines this relationship, often requiring careful negotiation and compromise to maintain stability and productive engagement.

The relationship with China has grown significantly in recent years, driven primarily by China's expanding economic influence in the region and its investments in Bangladesh's infrastructure projects under the Belt and Road Initiative (BRI). China's substantial investments in infrastructure, including ports, power plants, and transportation networks, have significantly impacted Bangladesh's economic development trajectory. However, policymakers must carefully consider concerns about debt sustainability and potential geopolitical implications of China's growing influence. Balancing economic gains with strategic considerations is essential in navigating this complex partnership.

Bangladesh's relations with other regional players, such as Pakistan and Myanmar, are marked by cooperation and challenges. Historical ties and shared religious heritage have influenced Bangladesh's relations with Pakistan, though differing strategic priorities and historical events have often presented obstacles. The Rohingya refugee crisis, arising from the violence in Myanmar, remains a major humanitarian and security challenge. Bangladesh has shouldered a significant burden in hosting the Rohingya refugees, straining its resources and presenting significant diplomatic and humanitarian dilemmas. Addressing this complex crisis requires a multifaceted approach that includes humanitarian aid and international pressure on Myanmar to find a lasting solution.

Furthermore, Bangladesh's expanding international footprint is evident in its engagement with several key global powers, including the United States, Japan, and European Union members. These partnerships provide access to development assistance, investment, and technology transfer, crucial for supporting Bangladesh's developmental objectives. Maintaining strong ties with these global powers enhances Bangladesh's diplomatic leverage and diversification of partnerships. This diversification of relationships is crucial to safeguarding Bangladesh's interests against potential external shocks and promoting balanced engagement in the international arena.

Bangladesh's foreign policy will likely continue expanding international ties, particularly as it strives to achieve its development goals and play a more prominent role on the global stage. The increasing integration of the Bangladeshi economy into global supply chains necessitates sustained engagement with international partners. However, challenges remain in managing the delicate balance between leveraging international relationships for economic development and safeguarding national interests. Furthermore, ensuring that international partnerships contribute to inclusive and sustainable development within Bangladesh remains a pivotal objective.

Bangladesh's success in managing its international relations will be crucial in determining its future development trajectory and its ability to meet the aspirations of its rapidly growing population. Successfully navigating the complex geopolitical landscape, managing relationships with major powers, addressing regional challenges, and balancing economic gains with strategic objectives will require skilful diplomacy, pragmatic decision-making, and a clear understanding of Bangladesh's national interests within the broader international context. The nation's ability to effectively integrate its foreign policy objectives with its domestic developmental agenda will be instrumental in shaping its future trajectory as a rising player on the world stage. Adapting to evolving global dynamics, strengthening institutional capacity for foreign policy management, and fostering greater public awareness about international affairs will further solidify Bangladesh's role in the international community.

The evolving international landscape, characterised by the rise of multipolarity and the growing significance of regional organisations, presents both opportunities and challenges for Bangladesh. Leveraging opportunities offered by the ever-increasing prominence of regional bodies like the BRICS and SCO, while maintaining its active participation in traditional multilateral forums such as the UN, will be vital for expanding its international influence and securing its economic interests. Navigating the complex dynamics of great power competition, especially between the United States and China, will require careful diplomacy and a nuanced approach prioritising Bangladesh's national interests.

In summary, Bangladesh's foreign policy is in a state of dynamic evolution. Its growing economic might and strategic ambitions drive its increased engagement with the global community. While challenges remain in managing complex regional relationships and balancing the interests of major global powers, Bangladesh's pragmatic approach to international relations, its commitment to multilateralism, and its increasing diplomatic dexterity position it well for navigating the complex international landscape and achieving its national objectives. The focus must remain on ensuring that the benefits of global engagement are effectively translated into sustainable development, social progress, and a better future for all Bangladeshis. The interplay between domestic development and foreign policy will define Bangladesh's future success and international role.

Chapter 7
Conclusion: Emerging Power Dynamics and Future Prospects

Assessing Emerging Power Dynamics within the Muslim World

The preceding chapters have presented detailed analyses of eight strategically significant Muslim-majority and Muslim-minority nations – Egypt, Türkiye, Pakistan, Indonesia, Malaysia, Nigeria, Iran, and Bangladesh – offering insights into their unique political trajectories, economic landscapes, military capabilities, and foreign policy orientations in 2025. This concluding section synthesises these findings, highlighting the emergent power dynamics shaping the Muslim world and their implications for global politics. A comparative analysis reveals both convergence and divergence in the paths these nations have taken, offering a nuanced understanding of the multifaceted nature of the contemporary Muslim world.

One striking commonality across these diverse nations is the enduring tension between religious identity and political governance. While the degree of influence exerted by religious institutions varies considerably—from the relatively secular state structures of Indonesia and Malaysia to the theocratic system of Iran—the interplay between religious beliefs, cultural norms, and political decision-making remains a defining feature in all eight cases. The challenge of balancing religious freedom with secular governance continues to shape political discourse and policy decisions, influencing everything from education policies to legal frameworks. The varying approaches adopted by these countries offer valuable case studies for examining how different societies grapple with this fundamental tension in the modern world.

Economic development presents another critical dimension, significantly varying trajectories and outcomes. Indonesia and Malaysia, for instance, have achieved notable economic progress, integrating successfully into the global economy and diversifying their export bases. In contrast, countries like Pakistan and Nigeria have struggled with persistent economic challenges, including high poverty levels, inequality, and dependence on volatile commodity markets. This disparity highlights the multifaceted nature of economic development, influenced by factors such as geographical location, resource endowments, governance structures, and global economic conditions. Analysing these contrasting trajectories reveals the complex interplay of internal and external factors influencing economic performance, providing lessons for understanding the challenges and opportunities faced by developing nations in the Muslim world.

These eight countries' military capabilities and modernisation efforts reveal a diverse landscape. Türkiye and Pakistan, for example, possess relatively robust military establishments and have actively pursued military modernisation programs, significantly influencing regional power dynamics. Countries like Bangladesh have adopted more modest approaches, prioritising economic development over expansive military expenditure. Strategic decisions regarding military spending reflect a nation's broader geopolitical priorities, financial constraints, and perceived security threats, demonstrating the complex relationship between internal development and external security.

Foreign policy orientations also present a spectrum of approaches. Some nations, such as Türkiye, have adopted increasingly assertive and independent foreign policies, seeking to expand their regional and international influence. Others, like Indonesia, have focused on promoting regional cooperation and multilateralism through organisations such as ASEAN. Different foreign policy stances reflect geopolitical ambitions, regional priorities, and historical experiences. The rise of non-Western alliances like BRICS and the SCO adds another layer of complexity, with these nations navigating their relationships with traditional and emerging global powers. This complex interplay shapes regional alliances, international partnerships, and power distribution on the world stage.

The relationship between these eight countries is equally complex and multifaceted. Historical ties, religious affiliations, geopolitical competition, and economic interdependence contribute to a dynamic and evolving web of interactions. Regional rivalries are evident, exemplified by the competition between Türkiye and Iran, or the historical tensions between Pakistan and India that spill over into regional alliances. Yet, these are also intertwined, participating in regional organisations, sharing resources, and engaging in diplomatic efforts to address shared concerns. The nuanced nature of these bilateral and multilateral relationships illustrates the complexities of regional politics within the Muslim world, where cooperation and competition coexist simultaneously.

Furthermore, the role of technology and its impact on these nations' development trajectories warrants careful attention. While some countries have successfully harnessed technological advancements for economic growth and social progress, others face challenges bridging the digital divide and fostering innovation. This disparity underscores the crucial role of infrastructure development, education reform, and investment in research and development for promoting sustainable economic growth. The differential adoption of technologies also highlights how global technological advancements interact with existing socioeconomic structures, influencing each nation's political and economic outcomes differently.

The rise of non-Western alliances, such as BRICS and the SCO, presents both opportunities and challenges for these eight countries. Membership in these organisations offers avenues for greater economic cooperation, resource access, and increased international influence. However, participation also necessitates navigating complex geopolitical landscapes and balancing relationships with traditional and emerging global powers. The choices these nations make regarding their engagement with these alliances will have profound implications for their future development trajectories and regional influence.

In conclusion, the Muslim world in 2025 presents a mosaic of diverse trajectories. While common themes such as the interplay between religious identity and governance, economic development challenges, and the evolving role in global politics bind them, the specific experiences of these eight countries reveal a diverse range of approaches and outcomes. The power dynamics within the region are fluid and complex, shaped by a confluence of historical legacies, domestic political structures, economic opportunities, and evolving global partnerships. Understanding these intricate interactions is crucial for comprehending the future trajectory of the Muslim world and its impact on the worldwide stage. The analysis presented in this book provides a framework for understanding this multifaceted landscape, suggesting areas for further research and highlighting the importance of nuanced and comprehensive analysis when considering these dynamic and evolving societies. The ongoing need to address internal challenges and navigate the complexities of international relations will continue to define the development trajectories of these nations and their roles in shaping the geopolitical landscape of the 21st century. The continued interplay between domestic priorities and the global arena, as well as the adaptation to changing alliances and power dynamics, will be critical in determining these essential global players' future success and standing.

The Evolving Influence of Muslim Majority Countries on the Global Stage

The evolving influence of Muslim-majority countries on the global stage is a complex and multifaceted phenomenon, shaped by a confluence of factors ranging from their internal political and economic dynamics to their engagement with international organisations and their responses to global challenges. While generalisations about such a diverse group of nations are inherently risky, specific trends and patterns emerge when analysing their collective impact on the world stage. Their positive and negative contributions extend across various sectors, from economic development and humanitarian aid to conflict resolution and promoting interfaith dialogue.

One significant aspect of their global influence stems from their participation in and contributions to major international organisations. For instance, the Organisation of Islamic Cooperation (OIC) is a prominent platform for these nations to address issues of common concern, including religious freedom, human rights, and the resolution of inter-state disputes. While its effectiveness has been debated, the OIC provides a unique forum for collective action and diplomatic initiatives, often focusing on issues that might not receive adequate attention within the broader framework of the United Nations. The OIC's humanitarian aid and disaster relief initiatives have supported communities in need, demonstrating a capacity for collective action within the Muslim world. However, the OIC's internal dynamics and occasionally divergent national interests can sometimes hinder its effectiveness in achieving its stated goals.

Furthermore, many Muslim-majority countries hold significant membership in the United Nations and its various agencies. Their participation in the UN General Assembly, Security Council (in the case of some countries), and other specialised agencies provides them with platforms to advocate for their interests, shape global agendas, and contribute to international decision-making processes. Their voting patterns and diplomatic actions within the UN system reflect their unique perspectives and priorities, often influencing discussions on issues ranging from climate change and sustainable development to peace and security. The influence of these nations within the UN usually depends on factors such as their economic clout, diplomatic skills, and ability to build alliances with other member states.

Beyond formal international organisations, Muslim-majority countries exert influence through bilateral and multilateral partnerships, contributing significantly to global economic development. Several nations have actively engaged in South-South cooperation, sharing experiences, resources, and expertise with other developing countries, particularly within their regions. This form of collaboration often bypasses the traditional North-South dynamics, fostering greater equity and mutual benefit. Indonesia, for instance, plays a crucial role in regional development through its engagement with ASEAN, while Türkiye's expanding economic ties across Africa and the Middle East demonstrate its increasing financial leverage. These initiatives often involve infrastructure development, trade agreements, and technology transfer, fostering economic growth and interdependence.

However, the influence of Muslim-majority countries is not without its complexities and challenges. Internal political instability, economic disparities, and ongoing regional conflicts often hinder their collective ability to exert unified influence on the global stage. Furthermore, the perception of Islam in the West and the rise of Islamophobia have created an environment of mutual misunderstanding and distrust, often impacting international relations and cooperation. This usually results in prejudiced policy decisions concerning these states, leading to various international injustices and misinterpretations of their actions and goals.

The issue of terrorism and the association of certain extremist groups with Islam cast a long shadow over the global perception of these countries. Although the vast majority of Muslims condemn terrorism unequivocally, the actions of a small minority have had a disproportionately negative impact on the global image of the Muslim world. This, in turn, has led to increased scrutiny and sometimes discriminatory practices affecting individuals and communities affiliated with Islam across the globe. Addressing this challenge requires ongoing efforts to counter extremist ideologies and promote moderate voices within the Muslim world, fostering a global dialogue based on mutual understanding and respect.

Moreover, the differing levels of economic development across Muslim-majority countries contribute to variations in their global influence. While some nations have achieved remarkable economic progress, integrating effectively into the global economy, others struggle with persistent poverty, inequality, and limited resource access. This economic disparity shapes their ability to engage actively in global initiatives and influence international affairs. Addressing this internal economic disparity within these nations is critical for enhancing their collective ability to participate more effectively in global governance and partnerships.

The rise of non-Western alliances, such as BRICS and the Shanghai Cooperation Organisation (SCO), presents opportunities and challenges for Muslim-majority countries. Participation in these groups can enhance their economic and political influence, fostering South-South cooperation and providing alternative platforms for engagement in global affairs. However, it also requires navigating complex geopolitical landscapes, balancing relationships with traditional and emerging global powers, and addressing potential internal conflicts of interest. This necessitates strategic planning and adaptability to the evolving geopolitical situation.

Looking ahead, the future influence of Muslim-majority countries on the global stage will depend on several interconnected factors. These include their ability to address internal challenges, such as political instability, economic disparities, and social inequalities; their capacity to build strong, inclusive institutions; their willingness to engage constructively in international cooperation and diplomacy; and their ability to foster a more nuanced and accurate global perception of Islam. Furthermore, the evolving geopolitical landscape, including the rise of new power dynamics and the ongoing challenges of international security and climate change, will profoundly impact their collective capacity to exert influence.

Successfully navigating these challenges and opportunities will require proactive governance, strategic decision-making within individual nations, and a renewed focus on collective action and collaboration within the Muslim world. Fostering greater unity and mutual understanding among these diverse nations, while respecting their unique identities and priorities, is paramount for enhancing their collective voice and influence on the global stage. The ability of these nations to cooperate effectively on international issues, such as climate change, terrorism, and economic development, will significantly contribute to their future standing and potential to shape a more just and equitable world. The focus must be on leveraging their collective strengths while simultaneously addressing internal and external challenges through diplomacy, collaboration, and mutual understanding. The path towards a more prominent role on the global stage necessitates internal stability, effective governance, and an unwavering commitment to promoting peace, development, and international cooperation.

Challenges and Opportunities for the Future Forecasting Future Trends

The trajectory of Muslim-majority and Muslim-minority countries in the coming decades hinges on a complex interplay of internal and external factors. Forecasting future trends requires a nuanced understanding of these interwoven dynamics, acknowledging the potential for significant progress and the persistence of considerable challenges. Political stability, a cornerstone of sustained development, remains a critical concern for many nations. Internal conflicts, ethnic tensions, and the struggle for political legitimacy plague several regions, diverting resources from crucial development initiatives and undermining economic progress. The capacity of governments to establish credible and inclusive political systems, guaranteeing fair representation and protecting human rights, will directly influence their long-term stability and ability to engage effectively with the global community. Strengthening democratic institutions, promoting good governance, and ensuring the rule of law are prerequisites for sustainable development and attracting foreign investment. Failure to address these internal political challenges will likely perpetuate cycles of instability and hinder economic growth, ultimately limiting their global influence.

Economically, the prospects are diverse and depend significantly on individual countries' resource endowments, policy choices, and integration into the global economy. While some nations are well-positioned to benefit from international trade and investment, others face significant hurdles, including limited diversification of their economies, dependence on natural resources, and persistent poverty. Diversifying economic activities, developing robust infrastructure, and investing in education and human capital are crucial for sustainable economic growth. Furthermore, adopting innovative technologies and policies promoting entrepreneurship and job creation will ensure inclusive and equitable development. The effective management of natural resources, coupled with a commitment to sustainable development practices, will be essential to avoiding environmental degradation and ensuring long-term economic prosperity. Failing to address these financial challenges could increase social unrest and mass migration, exacerbating existing inequalities and undermining political stability.

Social development, encompassing education, healthcare, and gender equality, is intrinsically linked to political stability and economic progress. Improving access to quality education, particularly for girls and women, fosters human capital development and empowers marginalised communities. Investing in healthcare infrastructure and promoting public health initiatives will contribute to a healthier and more productive workforce. Addressing social inequalities, promoting gender equality, and protecting the rights of minorities are crucial for building cohesive and resilient societies. The failure to address these social issues could lead to social fragmentation, hindering national unity and economic development, consequently diminishing their influence on the international stage.

Technological advancements present both opportunities and challenges for these countries. The rapid proliferation of digital technologies offers the potential for economic growth, enhanced communication, and improved access to information. However, these technologies also pose risks, including the spread of misinformation, cyber threats, and the widening digital divide. The ability of these nations to harness the benefits of technology while mitigating its risks will be critical to their future development. Strategic investments in digital infrastructure, coupled with policies promoting digital literacy and cybersecurity, will be necessary to fully realise the potential of technology for sustainable development. Ignoring this technological landscape could lead to them falling behind their peers, diminishing their potential to participate fully in the globalised world.

The geopolitical landscape also presents both opportunities and challenges. The rise of non-Western alliances, such as BRICS and the SCO, offers these countries the potential for increased economic and political influence, providing alternative global engagement platforms. However, navigating the complex relationships between these alliances and traditional Western powers will require careful diplomacy and strategic planning. The ability to leverage these new partnerships while maintaining constructive relations with conventional partners will be crucial to maximising their influence on the global stage. A failure to effectively navigate this geopolitical shift could lead to isolation, limiting their potential for economic growth and political influence.

The ongoing challenges of global security, including terrorism, climate change, and pandemics, pose significant threats to the stability and development of these countries. Effectively addressing these challenges will require cooperation and coordination among nations. Participating actively in international efforts to combat terrorism, mitigate climate change, and manage pandemics will be critical to protecting their populations and promoting long-term development. A failure to engage constructively in these global challenges could result in heightened security risks, economic instability, and social disruption, ultimately hindering their progress.

The future influence of Muslim-majority and Muslim-minority countries on the global stage will depend crucially on their ability to address these internal and external challenges effectively. Success will require strong leadership, effective governance, inclusive policies, and a commitment to sustainable development. Strengthening democratic institutions, fostering economic growth, promoting social inclusion, and adapting to technological advancements are all essential components of this process.

Effective engagement with the international community through multilateral institutions and bilateral partnerships will also be crucial for maximising their influence and realising their potential to shape a more just and equitable world. The willingness to address global challenges through collaboration and cooperation will be equally important.

The coming years will be critical for these nations, a time of significant opportunity and considerable risk. Their chosen path will determine their future and contribution to the global landscape. Their success in navigating these challenges and capitalising on opportunities will depend on a combination of factors, including leadership, policy choices, and the ability to adapt to a rapidly changing world. Developing resilient economies, stable political systems, and cohesive societies will ensure their future prosperity and continued influence on the world stage. Ultimately, their ability to leverage their strengths, address their weaknesses, and engage effectively with the global community will shape their future trajectory and impact on the international order. It is crucial to move beyond simplistic generalisations and engage in a deeper, more nuanced understanding of Muslim diversity to forecast future trends accurately. We can only effectively appreciate these nations' potential contributions and challenges to the global community.

The Role of Technology and Innovation Shaping Future Trajectories

The transformative power of technology and innovation is reshaping the political, economic, and social landscapes of Muslim-majority and Muslim-minority countries, presenting both unprecedented opportunities and significant challenges. The digital revolution, characterised by the rapid proliferation of mobile technologies, the internet, and artificial intelligence, fundamentally alters how these nations function, interact, and engage with the global community. This section delves into the multifaceted implications of this technological shift, exploring its impact on various sectors and considering the specific contexts of the countries under consideration.

One of the most profound impacts of technology is its potential to drive economic growth. In countries like Indonesia and Bangladesh, with large populations and a burgeoning young workforce, mobile banking and e-commerce platforms can revolutionise financial inclusion, extending access to credit and financial services to previously underserved populations. This could unlock significant entrepreneurial activity and foster economic growth by empowering small and medium-sized enterprises (SMEs), which constitute the backbone of many of these economies. Similarly, adopting precision agriculture techniques, facilitated by drones and satellite imagery, can significantly improve agricultural yields, enhance food security, and contribute to economic development in predominantly agrarian societies like Pakistan and Nigeria.

However, the path to technological progress is not without its obstacles. The digital divide remains a significant barrier to equitable access to technology and its benefits. Unequal access to internet infrastructure, digital literacy, and technological skills creates disparities within these countries, potentially exacerbating existing social and economic inequalities. Addressing this divide requires significant investment in infrastructure development, digital literacy programs, and initiatives promoting STEM education to equip citizens with the necessary skills to thrive in a digitally driven economy. Furthermore, the effective regulation of the digital economy is paramount to preventing the exploitation of vulnerable populations and ensuring responsible technological development.

The influence of technology extends far beyond the economic sphere. Social media platforms have become powerful tools for political mobilisation and social activism. These platforms can facilitate the dissemination of information, organise protests, and amplify the voices of marginalised communities. In countries grappling with political repression, social media has emerged as an essential tool for circumventing state censorship and fostering public discourse. However, this power also presents risks, including the spread of misinformation, the erosion of trust in traditional institutions, and the potential for online radicalisation and violence. Governments must develop strategies to manage the risks associated with social media while preserving freedom of expression and protecting vulnerable populations from online harm.

Furthermore, the rapid advancement of artificial intelligence (AI) presents opportunities and challenges. AI-powered systems can be utilised to improve healthcare outcomes, optimise resource allocation, and enhance public safety. The application of AI in areas such as disease surveillance, personalised medicine, and disaster management can significantly improve the quality of life and strengthen resilience to global challenges like pandemics and climate change. However, the ethical implications of AI must be carefully considered. Concerns around algorithmic bias, data privacy, and the potential for job displacement necessitate the development of robust ethical guidelines and regulatory frameworks to ensure responsible AI development and deployment.

The military applications of technology are also transforming the security landscape. The development of advanced weaponry, surveillance technologies, and cyber warfare capabilities has significantly altered the dynamics of regional conflicts. Many of these countries invest heavily in military modernisation, leading to an arms race that could destabilise the region. The effective management of this technological competition requires a proactive approach to arms control, fostering dialogue and promoting transparency in military procurement and development.

The geopolitical implications of technology are equally significant. The rise of digital platforms and global connectivity has created new avenues for international cooperation and idea exchange. However, it also presents the risk of cyber warfare, economic espionage, and interference in domestic affairs. These countries must navigate this complex landscape by strengthening their cybersecurity infrastructure, developing robust national strategies to counter cyber threats, and cooperating with international partners to address these transboundary challenges.

Examining the case of Türkiye reveals a complex interplay between technological advancement and national development. Türkiye has made significant strides in areas such as telecommunications, fintech, and the development of drone technology. However, the country also faces challenges related to digital literacy, cybersecurity, and the potential for technological tools to be used for surveillance and repression. Similarly, Indonesia, a large and diverse archipelago, is leveraging technology to address infrastructure development, economic inclusion, and healthcare delivery challenges. However, the country needs to address issues related to digital inequality and effectively regulate the rapidly growing digital economy.

The Role of Technology and Innovation Shaping Future Trajectories

Pakistan, a country with a large and growing population, faces significant challenges in terms of infrastructure development and technological capacity. The government has the potential to leverage technology to improve education, healthcare, and economic opportunities, but significant investments in human capital and infrastructure are required to realise this potential fully. With substantial economic potential, Nigeria faces challenges related to power infrastructure and the digital divide. However, the country also has a thriving tech sector and the potential to leverage technology to drive economic growth and improve the lives of its citizens.

These examples highlight the varied ways in which technology is shaping the trajectories of Muslim-majority and Muslim-minority countries. Successful integration of technology into national development strategies requires a holistic approach that addresses infrastructure, human capital, governance, and cybersecurity issues. Furthermore, these countries need to foster an environment that encourages innovation, promotes entrepreneurship, and protects the rights and safety of their citizens in the digital age. A failure to effectively manage this technological transformation could exacerbate existing inequalities, limit economic growth, and threaten social stability. Conversely, the strategic adoption of technology can unlock transformative opportunities and empower these nations to play a greater role in shaping the future of the global community.

In conclusion, technology and innovation are not simply tools for development; they are fundamental drivers of change, shaping the political, economic, and social landscapes of Muslim-majority and Muslim-minority countries in profound ways. Their effective harnessing requires careful planning, investment in human capital, robust regulatory frameworks, and a commitment to addressing technological advancement's ethical and social implications. The future trajectories of these nations will be inextricably linked to their ability to navigate this technological revolution effectively, realising its transformative potential while mitigating its inherent risks. A nuanced understanding of this complex relationship is crucial for accurately forecasting their future influence on the global stage and for crafting effective strategies to support their sustainable development.

Recommendations for Policymakers and Researchers Guiding Future Actions

The preceding analysis underscores the multifaceted challenges and opportunities facing Muslim-majority and Muslim-minority nations in the evolving global landscape. Their trajectories are intricately interwoven with technological advancements, economic shifts, and shifting geopolitical alliances. To navigate this complex terrain effectively and foster sustainable development, policymakers and researchers must adopt a proactive and multifaceted approach. This necessitates a shift from generalised analyses to a deeper understanding of each nation's specific contexts and unique challenges.

For policymakers, the primary focus should be fostering strategic partnerships based on mutual respect and shared interests. This involves moving beyond transactional relationships towards collaborative frameworks that address common challenges and unlock synergistic opportunities. For instance, international collaborations addressing the digital divide could involve knowledge-sharing initiatives, joint infrastructure projects, and capacity-building programs. Developed nations could provide technical assistance and financial support to help bridge the gap in digital literacy and access to technology. This collaboration could be further strengthened through public-private partnerships that leverage the expertise of both government agencies and private sector technology companies.

Furthermore, policymakers must adopt a nuanced approach to security cooperation, acknowledging the legitimate security concerns of these nations while simultaneously promoting dialogue and conflict resolution mechanisms. This includes supporting initiatives to strengthen regional security architecture and promote non-proliferation efforts. Emphasis should be placed on collaborative efforts focused on countering terrorism and violent extremism, focusing on addressing the root causes of these phenomena through inclusive and sustainable development strategies. This may necessitate collaborative efforts to support education, economic empowerment, and the development of robust governance structures. Furthermore, promoting regional dialogue and diplomacy can help mitigate potential conflicts from competition for resources or ideological differences.

Financial assistance and development aid should be directed towards sustainable and inclusive development projects. This means moving away from solely focusing on macroeconomic indicators towards projects that directly benefit local communities and address pressing social challenges. Support for education, healthcare, infrastructure development, and small and medium-sized enterprises (SMES) should be prioritised. Transparent and accountable governance structures ensure that aid is effectively utilised and reaches the needy. The focus should be on building capacity and promoting self-reliance rather than creating dependencies. Aid packages could incorporate conditions that encourage good governance, respect for human rights, and economic transparency.

Addressing climate change is another crucial area in which international cooperation is needed. Muslim-majority and Muslim-minority nations are often disproportionately affected by climate change impacts, including droughts, floods, and rising sea levels. Collaborative efforts are required to develop climate-resilient infrastructure, promote sustainable agricultural practices, and support the transition to renewable energy sources. This includes providing technical assistance, financial support, and access to clean technologies. International initiatives can also be leveraged to foster knowledge sharing and capacity building in climate adaptation and mitigation.

In addition to these policy recommendations, researchers have a critical role in shaping a more informed and nuanced understanding of these nations. This involves conducting rigorous empirical research that moves beyond stereotypes and generalisations. Studies should focus on the diversity within these nations, exploring the complexities of their political systems, economic structures, and social dynamics. Research projects could delve into the lived experiences of different communities, providing insights into the challenges and opportunities marginalised groups face. This research can provide policymakers with the necessary evidence to develop effective and targeted policies.

Comparative studies of different countries within the region can help identify best practices and lessons learned. Researchers can offer valuable insights to inform policy decisions by comparing successful development strategies and exploring the factors contributing to political stability or instability. This comparative analysis should extend beyond simple economic indicators to include factors such as governance, social inclusion, and the role of civil society. By highlighting the successes and failures of different approaches, researchers can provide policymakers with valuable guidance in developing more effective development strategies.

Longitudinal studies that track changes over time are also critical. These studies can provide a deeper understanding of these nations' historical context and evolutionary trajectories. By studying the long-term effects of different policies and interventions, researchers can offer valuable insights into the effectiveness of other development approaches. Longitudinal research can also help to anticipate future trends and challenges, enabling policymakers to develop more proactive and responsive strategies.

Furthermore, research that explores the interaction between domestic and international factors is crucial. This includes examining the impact of global economic trends, geopolitical shifts, and technological advancements on these nations. Researchers need to understand how these external forces shape the internal dynamics of these countries and how these countries navigate the complexities of the global system. This necessitates a multi-disciplinary approach that draws on insights from political science, economics, sociology, anthropology, and other relevant fields.

The effective engagement of these nations requires a shift away from a purely Western-centric perspective. Researchers and policymakers must engage with local expertise and knowledge, drawing on insights from scholars and practitioners within these countries. This participatory approach can ensure that research findings are relevant and impactful. Involving local communities in research projects can also enhance data collection and ensure that research findings reflect the lived experiences of those most affected by development initiatives.

Finally, effective communication and knowledge dissemination are crucial. Researchers should actively engage with policymakers, civil society organisations, and the broader public to share their findings. This can help to bridge the gap between research and policy, ensuring that research findings inform decision-making and shape public discourse. Disseminating research findings through accessible formats, such as policy briefs, reports, and public lectures, can help to reach a wider audience and promote greater understanding of these complex issues.

In conclusion, navigating the complex realities of Muslim-majority and Muslim-minority nations requires a concerted effort from both policymakers and researchers. Adopting a proactive, collaborative, and nuanced approach can foster sustainable development, strengthen international cooperation, and build a more peaceful and prosperous future for these vital world regions. This necessitates a paradigm shift from generalised assumptions towards a deep understanding of each nation's unique challenges and opportunities, empowering them to shape their futures within a globalised context. The future of these nations is not merely a matter of regional significance; it holds global implications, requiring a sustained and collaborative engagement from the international community.

Acknowledgments

This project would not have been possible without the support, companionship, and thoughtful engagement of many individuals.

I am incredibly grateful to the many friends—Muslim and non-Muslim alike—whose curiosity, questions, reflections, and challenges inspired this work. Our conversations, whether over meals, on walks, or during moments of quiet contemplation, often evolved into dialogues that deepened my understanding and broadened my perspective.

To those with whom I have shared the rhythms of daily life—discussing, debating, worshipping, arguing, laughing, and learning together—you have helped shape the ideas in this book and the spirit in which they were written. Your openness, sincerity, and willingness to explore complex and sometimes uncomfortable questions were a source of genuine motivation throughout this journey.

To my family and close companions: thank you for your unwavering patience, encouragement, and love as I immersed myself in this demanding work.

Any faults or shortcomings that remain are entirely my own.

Glossary

ASEAN: Association of Southeast Asian Nations.

BRICS: Brazil, Russia, India, China, South Africa.

OIC: Organization of Islamic Cooperation.

SCO: Shanghai Cooperation Organisation.

SME: Small and Medium-sized Enterprises.

[

About Author

Dr. Shaikh Mohammad Shahriyar Wahab was born in Bangladesh and has lived, studied, and worked across Bangladesh, Saudi Arabia, New Zealand, and Australia. His journey through diverse cultural and religious landscapes has profoundly shaped his worldview and deepened his appreciation for the rich tapestry of human belief and practice.

He approaches religious differences with a spirit of openness and empathy, firmly believing in the importance of coexistence and harmonious community life. Driven by a deep curiosity, he actively engages in conversations with Muslims and non-Muslims, seeking to understand how others perceive Islam, worship, and the many questions, debates, and contradictions around faith and practice. He values these discussions not as points of division, but as opportunities for shared reflection and learning.

About Author

A medical practitioner by profession, Dr. Shahriyar Wahab is active in his field and continues to balance his professional responsibilities with his passion for learning and sharing ideas. He is especially drawn to exploring interpretations and insights, particularly those that challenge assumptions or invite deeper understanding. He is committed to fostering awareness and thoughtful engagement with knowledge that serves a broader human purpose. Through his writing and dialogue, he aims to offer readers meaningful, reflective perspectives rooted in a sincere pursuit of truth.

www.ingramcontent.com/pod-product-compliance
Lightning Source LLC
Chambersburg PA
CBHW020524080526
44583CB00013B/728